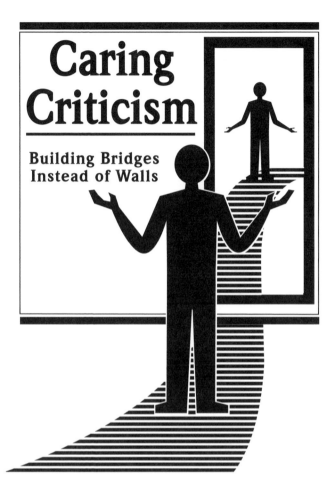

Caring
Criticism

**Building Bridges
Instead of Walls**

William J. Diehm

CARING CRITICISM

Published as part of the Care Classic® Series by Stephen Ministries.
Copyright © 1998 by Stephen Ministries. All rights reserved.
This edition licensed by permission of William J. Diehm. Previously
published in 1986 as *Criticizing* by Augsburg Publishing House.

Cover illustration: Joan Barnidge
Typesetting: Aleta Bird
Printing: Plus Communications

ISBN 0-8066-2211-3
Library of Congress Catalog Card Number 96-072144
Printed in the United States of America.

02 01 00 99 98
 5 4 3 2 1

Dedicated to my daughter-in-law,
Janice Crafton Diehm,
who motivated the idea,
edited the writing,
and taught me Ephesians 4:15:
to speak the truth in love.

Contents

Part One: Giving Criticism

Part Two: Receiving Criticism

Introduction

People need to learn ways to make their relationships more loving, honest, and lasting. That has not changed since this book was first published, nor since the first people carried on the first relationships. This is why I like this book, and why I am delighted Stephen Ministries is republishing it. *Caring Criticism* is a treasure chest full of ways to grow and deepen your most important relationships. It meets head-on a very challenging topic—giving and receiving criticism—and does so in a distinctively Christian and assertive manner.

A pastor and a psychologist, Dr. Diehm combines the Scriptures and sound psychological principles. I especially admire how he includes Christ as the head of all relationships. As Christ's love infuses relationships, whether one-to-one or in small groups, everyone benefits from the forgiveness, love, and authenticity that only Jesus brings.

Each time I read this book, I get more insight from it. Dr. Diehm shares his experiences from relationships on the homefront, in the classroom, and during counseling sessions to powerfully illustrate the wisdom God has given him. The result is a timeless work that will benefit many generations to come.

Through the Care Classic Series, Stephen Ministries is proud to republish this previously out-of-print book and to keep Dr. Diehm's teaching available. Books in the Care Classic Series are high-quality resources, theologically sound yet eminently practical and immediately applicable to daily living. They fill a definite need for individuals and congregations of all Christian denominations who are seeking quality resources to equip God's people for the work of ministry.

I thank God for Dr. Diehm's gifts of teaching, encouragement, and discernment. As you read and refer to *Caring Criticism* again and again, I know you will benefit from the way God works through Bill to bring us all closer together in Christian love.

Kenneth C. Haugk
Founder and Executive Director
Stephen Ministries

Foreword

Christian life—like all life—is dynamic. It has direction and involves growth. "Instead, by speaking the truth in a spirit of love, we must grow up in every way to Christ, who is the head" (Ephesians 4:15 TEV). God *calls* us to grow. "Grow in the grace and knowledge of our Lord and Savior Jesus Christ" (2 Peter 3:18). We grow in what God has given us—the grace of being in a relationship with him.

Christian growth is both personal and corporate. Living in interdependence with others, we grow within the Christian community—the body of Christ. This growth is the work of the Holy Spirit. Paul spelled it out clearly: "The fruit of the Spirit is love, joy, peace, patience, kindness, goodness, faithfulness, gentleness and self-control" (Galatians 5:22).

Although the analogy is from nature's growth from blossom to fruit, Christian growth is not completed in our lifetime. We are always moving, but never arriving. Actually we grow in our *awareness* of our need for growth. And Christian growth may not be as observable to the senses as is nature's fruit. It is patterned after the crucifixion and resurrection of Christ. The experience is seldom steady and gradual. The way up may be the way down. The new comes out of the death of the old.

Christian growth is therefore a venture of faith that focuses on forgiveness. It happens in response to God's call and is secured only by God's grace.

God calls us to grow by creating within us a desire for it. "As a deer longs for a stream of cool water, so I long for you, O God" (Psalm 42:1 TEV). Peter also described this desire: "Crave pure spiritual milk, so that by it you may grow up in your salvation, now that you have tasted that the Lord is good" (1 Peter 2:2). Jesus described it as "hungering and thirsting." "Blessed are those who hunger and thirst for righteousness, for they will be filled" (Matthew 5:6).

This book is intended to help this pilgrimage of growth. Growth takes place in interaction with the human community. It involves not only our relationship with God but also our relationship with people. In this book psychologist William J. Diehm provides guidance in a particularly hazardous activity in this community—criticizing. Some have been devastated by it; others have been blessed by it. There is a knack to giving it and to receiving it.

With his gentle approach Diehm first helps us to decide whether criticism will help or hinder and then how to prepare ourselves and others for giving and receiving it, should we decide to do so. His perceptive insights into human functioning help us understand our own and others' defensiveness as we attempt to be more open as persons. We are in a position then to utilize the influence of others for our growth.

William E. Hulme

Preface

When I was five years old, I contracted poliomyelitis. It gave me one year of excruciating pain and two lifeless legs. I wore braces on both legs and on my back and walked with great difficulty, pulling myself around with crutches. As a youngster, I remember watching the neighborhood kids playing ball on a sandlot next door. They laughed and jeered at me, saying, "What are you lookin' at, kid? Get lost. We don't want any crips around here."

My eyes welled with tears as I dragged my recalcitrant body into a shed behind our home where my father stored coal. I remember sitting on top of that pile of coal crying and swearing and hitting the tin-plated sides of the coal bin with my fists, calling myself every name I could think of. I hated myself for being crippled, and at that moment, I didn't want to live anymore.

Hearing my crying and banging and swearing, my mother marched across the lawn and stuck her head into the dark coal bin. In a stern voice, she said, "Billy, you come into the house this instant."

My whole body jerked, tumbling my crutches to the floor. "Yes, Mom," I said, figuring I was really going to get it for swearing.

I finally managed to perch myself on a high stool in our kitchen, bracing myself with my crutches. I was covered with coal dust and my face was streaked with black tears. My mother busied herself at the kitchen sink, washing dishes and setting them out to be rinsed and dried. After what seemed to be a millennium, she turned to me. "Billy, your father and I have given you the best kind of home we know how."

I sobbed and replied, "Yeah, Mom, I know we have a good house."

"What would you say if one of the neighbor kids called your home a dirty, filthy pigpen?"

"I wouldn't let anybody call my house a dirty, filthy pigpen," I replied.

My mother smiled softly and said, "Son, I don't know why God has given you a crippled body, but evidently it's best for you right now. It's the house in which you have to live, and it's time you quit calling it a dirty, filthy pigpen."

I have experienced the terrible feeling of self-loathing that can grow and consume a child who is different from other people, who feels rejected and scorned and criticized. I have also experienced the terrible feeling of depression and negativism that overpowers happiness when a person fights rejection by becoming a skeptical critic.

The greatest battle of my life has not been with polio but with criticism. The number one problem expressed by people who come to see me for counseling has been their inability to cope with criticism. Something my clients do not know is that they themselves have difficulty talking to people without using a harmful, critical approach. It is so easy to recognize bitter criticism when it is directed toward me. It is not easy to recognize harmful criticism when I am directing it toward you.

Learning how to cope with criticism is a survival art. It

is no less an art to learn how to correct and interact with people without using criticism. This book has grown out of my own experiences in learning how to help people change without hurting them or making them angry, and learning how to listen to people without taking offense and being crushed.

I wish I could say that I have mastered all negative response to criticism and that I no longer feel critical of myself or others. Criticism still hurts me and sometimes discourages me. I am still troubled by my tactlessness and how it sometimes hurts others. But I have improved. I am learning how to handle negative criticism in a positive way. I am learning to be my own cheerleader, and I am learning how to help other people change without arousing resentments. I am eager to share some of the lessons I have learned in the art of giving and surviving criticism.

Part One of this book discusses how we can learn to give criticism or correction to others in ways that are nonthreatening and helpful. Part Two shows how we can find positive ways to respond when criticism is directed at us.

The names of persons and details of experiences from my own life and counseling practice have been changed to protect privacy.

Part One
Giving Criticism

1
Why Criticism Doesn't Work

Criticism has caused more unhappiness, shattered more marriages, destroyed more children, discouraged more people, and stopped more progress than any other weapon. Even God doesn't like it. When the children of Israel were wandering through the wilderness on the way to the promised land, their faultfinding, complaints, and critical attitude gave God a heartache, and almost terminated the journey (Exodus 32:9-10).

Often we fall into the habit of criticism without realizing how destructive our sharp-tongued words really are. In his best-selling book, *How to Win Friends and Influence People,* consultant and author Dale Carnegie titled the first chapter, "Don't Criticize, Condemn, or Complain." When I worked for Mr. Carnegie, I asked him, "Why did you start your book with the negative, 'Don't Criticize'?"

He replied, "I thought and thought, but I could find no other way of saying the most important idea of dealing

3

with people. That idea is—don't criticize."

I asked him why he felt this rule was so important in human relations. He replied, "Criticism hurts people's feelings. It puts people down. It makes people depressed. It starts a fight, and it destroys relationships."

In this book the word *criticism* means unfavorable remarks or judgments, faultfinding, blame, disapproval, reproof, or censure. (I am not considering the use of criticism as the art or science of making careful judgments on the merits and faults of books, music, plays, acting, or other literary or artistic works.) Simply stated, criticism is when one person finds fault with another in a judgmental way.

Critical words can destroy our will to live. Criticism looks at what is wrong, and then, with bitterness and sarcasm, calls it to the other person's attention.

A first-grade teacher experimented with the idea that children live up to expectations and live down to criticism. She divided the children in her class into those who had brown eyes and those who had blue eyes. Then she told everyone that brown-eyed children were inferior. As a result, the brown-eyed children began to misbehave, get poorer grades, and assume the role of lower-status children.

This teacher then turned the game around and began criticizing the blue-eyed children. She said that a mistake had been made, and that brown-eyed children were actually more intelligent than blue-eyed children. A startling reversal of roles, grades, and behavior revealed that criticism hurts more than most of us imagine.

Over the past half-century, I have counseled more than 50,000 people. I have discovered that when a person has low self-esteem, a self-defeating attitude, and an inability to cope, it almost always stems from early childhood experiences and memories of critical attacks from others.

At the UCLA Medical Center an attempt was made to discover why some children were slow learners. The researchers placed problem children in a room in which they could be observed interacting with their mothers. They also observed interaction of well-adjusted children as they played with their mothers.

When a problem child played a game with his or her mother and made a mistake, the mother responded with words such as, "You're stupid! You don't know anything!" When a well-adjusted child played with his or her mother, the mother would say, "What's this, honey?" If the child didn't know, the mother would explain, "It's a sled. See, it goes on the snow like this. You remember when we went sledding last year." Mothers of well-adjusted children explained; they seldom criticized. The mothers of problem children criticized; they seldom explained. Criticism is especially discouraging when it comes from those we love most.

In Revelation 12:10, Satan is called the "accuser of our brothers." Accusation and criticism are Satan's chief weapons. When the sons of God presented themselves before the heavenly throne (Job 1:6), the devil was there to criticize the human beings on earth. The book of Genesis tells how he began his approach to Adam and Eve by criticizing God. The book of Revelation depicts Christ riding a white horse with the sword of the Spirit coming from his mouth. This symbolizes the final defeat of the stinging words of Satan by the Word of Christ. Whenever we pick up a weapon that Satan uses to fight and destroy—such as criticism—we endanger ourselves because that weapon is on his side.

Encouragement is a tool. Criticism is a weapon. A weapon is to be used only with great care and when all else fails. Even then, criticism divides and destroys like a pillaging army. Criticism simply doesn't work because it hurts people's feelings; they feel put down and lose self-esteem. Criticism discourages people and often depresses them. It starts fights, destroys relationships, and attracts evil influences to itself. Criticism is a half-truth that focuses on bad news, creates a negative atmosphere, and destroys the love that binds together the family, the community, and the church.

It is for these reasons that I pass on to you the simple but valuable advice, "Don't criticize!" Later in this book we will see how to replace negative criticism with the positive process of correction.

2
Why Do We Criticize?

There's a positive and negative side of criticizing. When I criticize someone else, I think of it as positive—I tell myself that I'm doing it out of love for others. However, when I am being criticized, I think of it as negative—I feel as if the person who is doing it is just being cruel. However, there is more to it than just my own personal feelings. Let's look at the positive and negative dynamics of criticizing.

Positive reasons why we criticize

A sign of love and commitment

Parents are naturally concerned about the behavior of their children. Good parents want to improve and direct the behavior of their children, so it is easy for them to get into the habit of correcting errors. But if the only time children get attention from their parents is when they do something wrong, they may learn that misbehaving is the best way for them to obtain attention.

The psychological approach called Transactional Analysis suggests that there is a parent, an adult, and a child who live within each of us. When we correct another person on an adult-to-adult basis, the criticism seldom causes offense, but a correction that comes from a parental position of authority can hook the child within us all and elicit an angry response. According to Transactional Analysis, if we remember not to criticize others in such a way that we put them down by our criticism, we will seldom hurt them. And if we remember that other people are sometimes inclined to come down on us from a superior, parent position, we may be able to accept the type of criticism that otherwise would make us angry.

It is not unusual for an interchange between a parent and a child to sound like this:

"Stop that," says the parent in a harsh voice.

"Why?" asks the child in an inquiring, defiant way.

"Because I said so," the parent responds angrily.

Such an interchange puts the parent in a dominant position and the child in an inferior position, regardless of whether the child is right or wrong.

To keep from putting the child down, the parent could explain why the child should "stop that." Even if the reason is "You are irritating me and making me angry" or "I can't stand your behavior," at least that would let the child know that the reason the parent wants him or her to stop is personal irritation. The parent's words would then not be just a put-down.

Sometimes we need to correct people in order to live with them successfully; but if our correction is not done with love and consideration, it can easily have negative results.

Most of us are reluctant to accept criticism from strangers, probably because love and commitment are not likely to exist. We are also reluctant to accept correction from family members unless we are sure that it comes to us in a loving, concerned way.

The first way I remember getting criticized was in my cradle by the hand of my father. His swats on my diaper were informing me that I was to sleep at night and stay awake in the daytime. People say that I was too young to remember, but I think I remember that episode. I also think it established a relationship between my father and me that made me fear his critical hand and withdraw from a loving relationship with him.

Now that I am a parent, I realize that parents correct their children in order to improve the children's behavior. But I believe parents are not careful enough in letting their children know that the correction is for the children's good and is being done in love. If parents can communicate the idea that they are correcting their children in order to help them, and not simply for their own convenience or out of petulance, then their children can grow up being less sensitive to criticism.

It is good that parents correct their children in order to teach them how to live more effectively and happily. But it is not good enough unless the children accept the idea that the correction is *for* them and not *against* them.

Once I reproved one of my grandchildren sharply. The child looked at me with a combination of questioning and hurt and said, "Grandpa, do you love me?"

Immediately I knew what I had done, and I replied, "Yes, I do love you, and that's why I told you that you must be on time for school. You are starting a bad habit that will last all your life and make things most difficult for you. Because I love you, I want to help you develop the habit of being on time."

Parents sometimes criticize children instead of correcting their undesirable behavior. If they instill fear of criticism in a child rather than an awareness of how the child's behavior should improve, they destine the child to great difficulty in being able to handle correction.

Marriage partners also often use criticism rather than correction. They justify their criticism by saying, "Because I love my spouse, I have to show him [or her] the right way to act." As a marriage partner you may want to help your spouse improve, but be sure you follow the principles of constructive correction and teaching. If you fall into the trap of criticizing, your partner will probably not cooperate very much in what you want him or her to do.

I have been a marriage counselor for a half-century, and if I were asked to identify the one thing that most contributes to divorce, I would say it is a *critical attitude*. At the beginning of a relationship, when a couple falls in love, there is truth to the saying that love is blind. Love decreases our sensitivity to the faults of others. At the early stages of romance, love can even turn idiosyncrasies and obnoxious habits into attractions.

Sensuality is often the fuel that keeps love burning between a man and a woman. But when the sensual attractions begin to fade, love loses some of its power, and the previously overlooked failings become a source of conflict. If a married couple has a critical spirit that leads them to rip other people apart for their failings, sooner or later they will surely turn on each other.

Why do marriage partners criticize each other? They do

it because one person does not like the behavior of the other person, and thinks that if the partner's behavior can be changed, it will increase his or her own happiness. The truth is that another person's behavior may be an *excuse* for our unhappiness, but it is not the *reason* for our unhappiness. We *choose* to be happy or unhappy. When a critical spirit comes upon a couple, and a husband lacerates his wife and she in turn flays him, the marriage is in the process of being destroyed. Very few people change as a result of having a critical tongue directed at them. When someone you love attacks you with a critical tongue, soften the impact of that criticism on you by remembering that the other person probably thinks he or she is expressing responsible love.

An honest concern for others

People also criticize out of honest concern for others. People are interested in those around them, and when they see something wrong with someone else, they have a desire to correct it. We groom each other and brush the lint off each other's collars. We tell people how to drive and where to park.

Correcting the failings in others seems to be built into the human race. We have a deep desire to improve ourselves and to correct the wrongs we see around us. We have a sense of fairness, a sense of rightness, a sense of the way things ought to be. God has written a sense of right and wrong into the secret place within us. Criticism springs to our lips when we see a violation of what we consider to be right.

We need to remember not to become too concerned when people mildly correct us. It's a part of their God-given instinct to try to improve things. The problem is a matter of degree. When people try to improve us too harshly or too often, it can become quite annoying and even harmful. It helps to remember that people naturally want to correct what appears to be wrong and are seldom being deliberately malicious when they criticize us.

One day I watched a man putting an outboard motor on his homemade boat. To protect the transom, he placed a rubber inner tube over it before he attached the outboard motor. I said to him, "Ted, there's too much power and vibration produced by your motor to have such a slippery cushion between the clamps and the transom." Ted didn't believe me and lost the motor in the lake. I helped him fish the motor out, clean it, and reclamp it. From then on, Ted listened to me a little more carefully. When you show an honest concern for people, and your criticism is justified, you can usually expect a happier ending.

A sense of responsibility

A third reason we criticize others is out of a sense of responsibility. Many people take responsibility very seriously, and when they find themselves in a position of authority, they try to shape up anyone who does not conform.

Good leaders know how they can get people to do what they want them to do without using harping, carping criticism. But some people aren't very good leaders. They rudely and crudely point out the mistakes and inconsistencies in others. If our boss makes us angry, he or she is probably only guilty of using bad management techniques, not of a desire to abuse us verbally. It may be easier for us to turn off our anger once we understand the motivation behind our boss's behavior.

We also need to realize that many people feel they need to be in charge. Naive people think being in charge means giving the orders, so they give orders. They search for any little thing they can call to our attention because they are under the mistaken notion that being critical means they are important.

A leader is automatically put into a position of giving advice, making suggestions, and correcting that which is being done in a nonproductive way. Leaders who accept their role in a good-humored way, exercise control over their critical comments, and prefer instead to inspire, will be leaders indeed. But if leaders view themselves as bosses, whose only method of correction is to call attention to the things they do not like, then they will have poor results in working with people.

When we are criticized, we can remember that those who are doing it often think criticism is an expression of responsibility. We do not need to overreact to those who criticize us only because they have not learned other methods of management or who do so because it makes them feel more important.

Negative reasons why we criticize

Low self-esteem

Critics often suffer from low self-esteem. Putting someone else down is a way people often try to bolster their own feelings of self-worth.

When I was a child, we played a game called "king of the hill." We would find some kind of a mound, like a dirt pile left by a contractor, and each of us would try to be the one who stood the highest on the hill. This was accomplished by shoving and pushing other people down.

Unfortunately there are still some people who think they can get ahead by forcing others down. "King of the hillers" may enter into a game of slander and gossip to destroy the reputation of the people ahead of them so they can assume their positions.

"King of the hill" is a very old technique. Absalom, the son of King David of Israel, played that game as he stood at the gates of Jerusalem talking to people about their grievances, saying, "If only I were king, I would make this terrible situation right." The "Absalom Technique" is used by politicians who think they will be elected by slandering their opponents. How I long to hear some candidate say, "Our president has done a marvelous job. He has made some mistakes, but by and large, we are all proud of him. I am running for office in the hope that I can do as good a job or perhaps better than our president, and I will try to make at least a new set of mistakes." I would vote for a candidate honest and strong enough to feel no need to play "king of the hill."

A cry for help

When I was a prison psychologist, inmates would often attack me with brutal, critical words. I have been called every name under the sun and moon. I have learned that a person who criticizes is not necessarily making a personal attack. Sometimes that person is ventilating helpless feelings or is involved in his or her own pain. Many times inmates who had begun by thoroughly criticizing me would end up crying and sobbing in my arms. Their attack on me was actually due to frustration, and in the end, it was an attack on themselves. What they really meant was, "Please help me. I'm hurting."

As a former pastor, I remember having a hard time with a particularly critical person in my church. My wife comforted me with words I will never forget. She said, "Bill, would you feel angry and hurt if she were blind?"

"Why, no," I replied.

"Well, in reality, Bill, she is blind. She has no idea how

to deal with people in a loving, uplifting way. She is blinded by bitterness and self-hate."

I knew my wife was right. So instead of responding angrily to my critic, I was able to see through the facade of her criticism and become aware that she was not really trying to hurt me. She was just responding to her own hurt.

Suffering people often defend themselves by projecting blame. Be wise enough to recognize that pain is often expressed in criticism of others. Whenever people criticize you in a loud, angry, strident tone, listen carefully. It may be that they are really asking for help.

An overdose of conformity

Critics often want other people to conform to their way of life so they will feel less frustrated and their lives will run more smoothly.

A man once said to me, "My wife is the complete opposite of me. When I say up, she says down. When I say black, she says white. Our tastes, attitudes, and behavior are as if we belonged to two different worlds."

I said to him, "Isn't it wonderful to live with someone who breaks the monotony by being different? How exciting to learn to live with and love someone who expands your horizons by bringing new ideas and new enjoyment to the marriage. You love hunting; she loves knitting. Now instead of just hunting or knitting, you have both hunting and knitting. You are a rich man."

A certain amount of conformity is a good thing in a marriage relationship because a husband and wife need to have some common values and viewpoints on which they can build for the future. But too often one or the other of them ends up with an "overdose" of conformity and refuses to allow the other person to be different. Life is enriched when we learn to appreciate the gifts and interests of others rather than insisting they think or act exactly the way we do.

Self-defense

One day while I was trying to help a young man solve his problems, he began to accuse me. "It's all your fault," he said. "If it wasn't for you, I wouldn't be this way."

The greatest problem any counselor faces is the failure of people to assume responsibility for their own problems. Their egos get in the way, and they blame others. Those who project fault on others are attempting to protect themselves from blame. The young man projected guilt on me so he could avoid taking responsibility for his own actions.

In psychology, the term *transference* defines that time in the psychological process when a client turns against the therapist; suddenly the therapist becomes a father or mother figure or someone who was responsible for the client's unhappiness. When patients work through transference and release their anger, they get better. But when they stop at that point, they may only leave therapy disliking the therapist, clinging to their old problems, and attacking others for the way they have chosen to be.

■ Summary

Why do we criticize? On the positive side, it may be because we are interested in others and desire to correct things that are wrong. Parents don't want their children to make the same mistakes they did, so they criticize. Employers think of criticism as a management tool. Some people think criticism is the only way to help change others.

Unfortunately, most critics do not realize how much criticism hurts—unless, of course, they are subjected to it themselves. Most critics suffer from low self-esteem. Many are insecure and become critical in order to protect themselves against criticism.

Some people are critics because they have developed the habit of being negative. In their attempt to correct others, they are honestly trying to improve them. But when we focus only on the negative, we let it grab the center stage. To harp on the negative gives one a negative attitude.

There are positive alternatives to the negative habit of criticizing. In the next chapter we will identify some of these.

3
If Criticism Doesn't Work, What Does?

What should we do when we want to help someone by giving them a suggestion or a bit of advice? Shouldn't we correct our children's behavior? Shouldn't we guide those who work for us? Are we to be totally accepting of every action around us? Of course not.

My suggestion is to use criticism rarely, if ever, and never if anything else will work. Like a bottle of nitroglycerine, criticism must be handled with great care.

It may be possible to justify criticism by pointing to certain biblical events that suggest we take a critical approach to sin. But a balanced, comprehensive reading of the Bible reveals that the prophets, teachers, and preachers in Scripture resorted to criticism only after they had explained, illustrated, and modeled the way of righteousness. When a prophet finally became critical, the flames of destruction were not far behind.

Jesus told us not to criticize. For example, in the Sermon on the Mount, he told us not to call anyone names (Matthew 5:22). He put it so strongly that he said if we call a person a fool, we are in danger of hellfire. In Matthew 7 we are told, "Do not judge, or you too will be judged." Calling other people names and judging them are two offensive ingredients of criticism.

If Jesus told us not to criticize, how can we account for his calling the teachers of the law and Pharisees hypocrites? (Matthew 23) That was indeed criticism. Jesus had been verbally attacked, however, by the scribes and Pharisees for three and a half years. He had used every method available to him to try to win them over, from winsome teaching to miracles. Nothing he had said or done had convinced them that the kingdom of God was at hand. Not until his ministry was over and he was ready to go to the cross and die for our sins did Jesus criticize the scribes and Pharisees. It was as if he knew criticism was the tool that would bring about his death. His opponents were looking for an offense in the life of a perfect man—which was difficult to find. When he criticized them, they found the offense. His criticism was what motivated them to find a way to destroy him.

It seems to me that when we are ready to go to the cross and have exhausted all methods of appealing to people through love and reason, then criticism may be a responsible approach. But we should remember that it might also get us killed, or at least deepen the division between us and others.

Instead of immediately using this technique of last resort that antagonized Jesus' enemies to the point of wanting to kill him, let's look at the methods Jesus used to encourage and give abundant life to millions.

Accepting the person

Jesus accepted individual people although he rejected much of their behavior. For example, Jesus kept Judas among his disciples, even though he knew Judas was stealing. He selected Matthew, even though he was a hated tax collector. He accepted Simon Peter, even after Peter's betrayal. The name Jesus means "he will save his people from their sins." God sent Jesus for the purpose of rescuing us from sin—but he did not accomplish this by using the method of criticism.

Another name for Jesus is Immanuel, which means "God with us" (Matthew 1:23). He did not reject even the most evil of persons. In fact the Bible tells us, "While we were still sinners, Christ died for us" (Romans 5:8). Jesus did not depend on criticism. Instead, he practiced acceptance.

Acceptance of others means that we believe in them, trust them, and care for them just as they are, even without their having made any changes. Acceptance says, "I may not like what you do, but I like you. You are my spouse [or child or friend], and even if you never change, I still love you." People are much more likely to change when we accept them in this way than they are if we criticize them and imply that we will hold back our love for them until they do what we want.

A woman came to me one day and said, "My husband has been unfaithful to me. I can never trust him again. And more than that, he has hurt me so badly that I just don't want to trust any man again."

What a terrible and unnecessary price this woman had chosen to pay for the sin that her husband had committed against her! Certainly she should not have taken his behavior lightly, and she had good reason to feel hurt and betrayed. His breach of her trust was a serious obstacle to the continuation of a healthy marriage relationship.

But this woman had gone far beyond that and had chosen to adopt a stance of rejection that posed an even greater threat to her marriage. Furthermore, she fully intended to use her husband's behavior as an excuse to hold a grudge against all men.

Such an attitude of rejection and distrust leaves no room for repentance, forgiveness, and reconciliation. It therefore makes relationships with other human beings impossible and condemns an individual to a life of judgmental loneliness. Just imagine the state we would be in if God had decided to deal with us the same way!

When you criticize someone, the result is often a counterattack. Accept, and you will be accepted; criticize and reject, and you will be criticized and rejected. We need to do as Jesus did—accept people unconditionally just as they are. If you want to see change take place in others, remember that it comes first of all from acceptance. If you cannot accept a person, then you cannot change him or her.

How do we accept another person? Start by focusing your mind on acceptance. Proceed by talking as if you accept him or her. Then allow feelings of acceptance to grow. And finally, act as if that person was someone you really love.

When I worked at Terminal Island Federal Penitentiary as a clinical psychologist, the inmates held a banquet in my honor and declared me "Inmate of the Year." I believe I received this high honor only because of my relationship with Jesus Christ, who taught me to accept people before I tried to change them.

I counsel hundreds of people every year. Almost always, they tell me of some terrible ogre in their life who is doing some awful things that they can't possibly accept. They go on to tell me that the more they talk to the ogre about his or her sins, the worse the ogre gets.

I often tell them that if they want to change someone

in their life, the first step is to accept the person and stop using negative verbalizations to try to make him or her conform. An attack on behavior can be successful only if we get the cooperation of the person who is misbehaving. People do not cooperate with those who do not accept them.

Friends accept us; enemies criticize us. We do not change for our enemies; we change for our friends. Criticism makes people feel worse; acceptance lets them know they are loved. When people know they are loved, they change from within. That is the method God uses, and I hope and pray that it will become our method as well.

Marriage counseling is my specialty, and I have studied to find methods of keeping people together. To me, criticism is Satan's number one tool to break up homes. Husbands and wives get into such a dreadful habit of criticizing each other that they erect a barrier of unhappiness between them. If you must criticize, do so before you marry. Afterwards, practice acceptance.

I know how difficult it is to accept some people. But the problem is that we are looking at their behavior, not at them as persons. If we criticize our children, it's because they have done something we don't like. Our aim should be to reject what we don't like (the behavior) and accept what we do like (the child).

Teaching what is right

Jesus could have begun the Sermon on the Mount with the words, "You evil people must realize that you need help." Instead he said, "Blessed are the poor in spirit, for theirs is the kingdom of heaven" (Matthew 5:3). In other words, happiness comes when you recognize that you are not perfect and that you need help.

One day a husband and wife came to see me for marriage counseling. The husband had been conducting one affair after another throughout their married life. His wife had caught him in another compromising situation and was deeply hurt. The man was defensive, claiming there was nothing wrong with his having sex with other women. He began to argue with me vigorously about his right to eat a variety of food, which was his rationalization for promiscuity. I opened a Bible and read the Ten Commandments to him as well as the first few chapters of the book of Proverbs. He was amazed and said, "I didn't know what I was doing was actually wrong."

Sometimes people do things we don't like because they simply don't know any better. If you teach them what is right, often people will automatically drop what is wrong. Wrong is wrong because it hurts. Right is right because it works.

One time I was the guest at a home where the father harshly criticized his son. He said, "You have the manners of a pig; you aren't fit to eat with normal people. Leave the table." The little boy was crushed under the harsh criticism of the father. I remembered that lesson, and I have made it a policy to call attention to the right way of doing things rather than to what the person is doing wrong. So when my son was eating with his fingers, I said to him, "John, eat with your fork as I am doing. It's easier, more polite, and healthier than eating with your fingers." I did not criticize his bad manners. I simply taught him better manners.

When I was a young man, I took the minister of our church for a ride in my car. I tried to impress him by driving too fast. I thought I was showing him what a good driver I was. I will never forget his crushing words at the end of the ride. "I can't possibly see how you can consider yourself a

Christian when you drive your car with such reckless disregard for the safety of others."

My pastor's words of criticism did not cause me to be a better driver, but a worse one. I actually drove faster and took more chances in a desperate attempt to get someone to compliment my great skill at high-speed driving. I stopped driving too fast when a patient person showed me how much better gas mileage I got, how much longer the car lasted, how much happier people were with me, and how much less stress was connected with careful driving.

Teaching a person the right thing to do is much better than criticizing him or her for doing something wrong. When we are persistent in teaching the truth, the truth itself becomes the best correction. There is no need to criticize. Truth is weapon enough.

Dialoging

Jesus dialoged with people and took time to answer their questions. Criticism judges quickly, and instead of dialoging, it argues. Jesus began his ministry as a little boy in the temple, asking and answering questions. Later he often allowed his opponents to interrupt his conversation and challenge him, and he freely debated with them in front of the crowd. At his trial, they asked him what he taught. He replied, "I have spoken openly to the world. I always taught in synagogues or at the temple, where all the Jews came together. I said nothing in secret" (John 18:20). Everything that Jesus said was said openly and was subject to debate.

A dialog allows an open relationship between people so that both sides can communicate their feelings and thoughts. A dialog gives people an opportunity to work negative ideas, feelings, words, and conduct out of their systems.

I remember telling my son Philip one day not to throw rocks at the swans in a pond. Later I looked up and saw him throwing rocks at the swans. I came up behind him, turned him over my knee, and spanked him. Afterward he explained to me through his sobs, "The big boys were trying to hurt the swans, and I was trying to get them to swim out in the lake so the big boys couldn't get them." Whether he was right or wrong, I don't know. But I will never forget how I jumped to a conclusion before I let him explain his side.

Once a woman from Syrian Phoenicia came to Jesus and asked him to heal her daughter. Jesus rebuffed her with the words, "It is not right to take the children's bread and toss it to their dogs" (Mark 7:27). He meant that God had given him a mission to the Jews, and her background did not allow her to interfere with that mission.

The woman replied, "Yes, Lord, but even the dogs under the table eat the children's crumbs."

Jesus accepted this beautiful dialog, healed her daughter, and declared that she had great faith.

In Isaiah 1:18 we read the words, " 'Come now, let us reason together,' says the Lord. 'Though your sins are like scarlet, they shall be as white as snow.' " That's God's method: reasoning together. No matter how far off base we think another person is, the way to resolution of the problem is through dialog and reasoning together.

As a Christian psychologist, I have discovered that one of the best methods for improving someone's mental attitude is dialog. Dialog consists of talk-listen, talk-listen. Most people can work out their problems if they have an opportunity to talk to someone with a sympathetic ear and an encouraging tongue.

A man was sent by his wife to my office for counseling.

She had said, "I can't live with him. His violent outbursts have put me into a state of perpetual fear. Why is my husband so angry?" At first he would not talk to me. His policy was to keep everything bottled up, and when the pressure got too great, he blew his cork. I got him to talk by practicing dialog psychotherapy. I just asked six questions:

1. *Why* are you so pressured?
2. *What* is bothering you?
3. *When* do you feel the pressure?
4. *Where* are you when it happens?
5. *Who* bothers you the most?
6. *How* do you express your anger?

These questions start a dialog. Listening to the answers continues it. Responding in a positive way completes the cycle.

I helped this man talk out his feelings and express his reasons for being so angry and frustrated. When he expressed himself and found a sympathetic ear and some encouragement, most of the answers came from him.

So when your child, spouse, neighbor, friend, employee, or employer is doing something that in your opinion is worthy of criticism—wait. First engage them in a dialog and ask questions that involve six words: *who, what, when, where, why,* and *how.* When you learn more about the situation, you may not want to criticize. You may even want to help.

Rewarding

Critics often end up rewarding negative behavior because that's what gets their attention. Jesus responded to positive behavior. When he was dying on the cross, he ignored the thief that chided him but he responded to the thief who asked him for help. When Herod asked Jesus to do a magic trick, Jesus ignored him; but when a man born blind asked for help, he restored his sight. Jesus often changed people's behavior by rewarding what was right and ignoring what was wrong.

In Educational Psychology courses, students learn about a process called *behavior modification.* B. F. Skinner, a noted researcher in this area, identified a technique that is called *operant conditioning.* His experiments with pigeons illustrate this technique. When you ignore a behavior you don't want and reward with grain a behavior you do want, a pigeon will abandon the unwanted behavior and continue the behavior you reward.

Animals can be trained to do almost anything when one reinforces desirable behavior by rewarding it and discourages undesirable behavior by ignoring it. When animals are rewarded for doing what their trainer wants them to do, they learn much more quickly than when they are punished for misbehavior.

What is true of animals is also true of human beings. Criticism is punishment. Praise is reward. If we really want people to change, we will praise them when they improve.

One day an angry woman brought her delinquent 15-year-old son to see me. In front of the sullen boy, the hostile mother bitterly complained about his recalcitrant behavior. I could feel the resentment in the air.

"Doesn't your son do anything right?" I asked.

"No, not a single thing!" she snarled.

Because the mother was too blind to see a single good thing in her own child, her son had no hope of any reward for doing something that pleased her. Constant tongue-lashing only makes a bad situation worse. It kills hope in people, and without hope they perish.

Our United States economy is based on the principle of

reward. Those who produce the highest quality product at the lowest possible cost are generally rewarded with success. Experience has shown that reward is an excellent motivator.

A man sought my advice about his son, who was borderline delinquent. He said that his son couldn't be depended on to do what he was told. I asked the father what he did when the boy disobeyed.

"I hit him," he said.

"What do you do when the boy obeys?" I asked.

"I don't do anything; that's what he's supposed to do," he responded.

"What do you do for a living?"

"I'm a carpenter."

"Suppose they assigned someone to hit you when you didn't frame a house correctly and to say nothing when you did. And, in either case, you received no paycheck."

"That's different. You're asking me to bribe my son," he replied angrily.

"No, I'm asking you to reward your son by complimenting him when he does the right thing. If you're going to ignore something, ignore his bad behavior, not his good behavior."

The father left my office convinced that his method was right and his son was wrong. I was not surprised when his son was sent to a juvenile correction facility for delinquency. In my opinion, it would have been more justified to send the father.

Correcting mistakes

The critic corrects people, not mistakes. Jesus corrected mistakes, not people.

The Sadducees tried to trap him by asking a trick question (Matthew 22:23-33). Jesus replied, "You are in error because you do not know the Scriptures or the power of God" (verse 29). He proceeded to correct their lack of knowledge, not them. When we criticize, our emphasis is almost always on the weakness of the person. Jesus talked about the weakness of the position.

As I write with a pencil on a piece of paper, I occasionally make a mistake. I reverse the pencil and erase the mistake. Then I redo the word and proceed.

Critics do not try to erase mistakes, they strive to blot out the person. When you blot out the person, there is no more writing. When you erase the mistake, the person has another chance.

One day Peter came to Jesus and asked, "Lord, how many times shall I forgive my brother when he sins against me? Up to seven times?"

Jesus replied, "I tell you, not seven times, but seventy-seven times" (Matthew 18:21-22). That was his way of saying errors are to be corrected. Peter was thinking in terms of correcting *people.* Jesus was thinking in terms of correcting *errors.* He was always pointing out God's will to his disciples and to others who would listen. And he constantly confronted people with the truth, correcting errors in thinking, faulty value systems, and sinful behavior. He corrected errors, but he accepted people.

One day when I was at work, my grandson borrowed our videocassette recorder. When he returned it, I still was not at home, so my wife Carrol attempted to reconnect the VCR. It didn't work. She had put a cord in a wrong spot. When I got home, she told me the television didn't work. I said, "Honey, this black cord connects to the antenna right here, not there."

I did not say to her, "Stupid, anyone can see that the cord goes there." I corrected the mistake, not her.

When a friend drove my car, he tried to pull the seat forward to fit his body. I said to him, "Greg, the switches for adjusting the seat are found to the left of you on the door panel." Greg didn't get angry at me any more than my wife did. They both simply said, "Oh," and did it the right way. If I had called them names or established blame, I would have been guilty of criticism instead of correction. Criticism would have ended in an angry confrontation; correction created a friendly change.

I formerly taught statistics classes at Azusa Pacific University. A few of my students were extremely inept at math. I could have called them names, insulting their intelligence and hurting their feelings. But I am certain they would have responded in kind, and in the end, they would have hated me and not learned statistics. I corrected their errors and had them do the assignment again. I didn't correct them, nor did I attack their egos. I wanted their egos and self-esteem to remain intact. Correction changes people, while criticism only makes them angry.

Encouraging

Critics establish blame. Jesus used encouragement. One of the last things Jesus said to his disciples was, "Surely I will be with you always, to the very end of the age" (Matthew 28:20). With these words he encouraged them.

It is easy to find other examples of Jesus motivating people to change through encouragement. John 8 tells of the woman caught in adultery who was brought to Jesus. He invited the person who had committed no sin to throw the first stone at her. One by one her accusers disappeared, beginning with the older ones. Jesus said to her, "Woman, where are they? Has no one condemned you?"

"No one, sir," she said.

"Then neither do I condemn you," Jesus declared. "Go now and leave your life of sin" (verses 10-11). He encouraged her as a person while disapproving of her sin.

Another time some men brought a paralytic to Jesus. Seeing their faith, Jesus said to the sick man, "Take heart, son; your sins are forgiven" (Matthew 9:2). Because sickness was often seen as a punishment for sin in those days, this would have been an especially encouraging word.

For several years I worked for a suicide-prevention clinic in San Pedro, California. There I learned that people sometimes attempt suicide when they have become discouraged, and that encouragement is the best weapon against self-destruction. Encouraging ideas can be expressed in words such as, "Things can change. It may seem all dark to you, but I see some exciting possibilities. I'll help you. We can do it." There are endless possibilities to use words of encouragement to help people.

My Aunt Dorothy was a writer. I loved the poems she wrote and the stories she told. I remember sitting with her at the old homestead, rummaging through a steamer trunk filled with the manuscripts she had written. She was going to burn them. I praised her writing, which as far as I know no one had ever done for her before. She had never submitted anything to a publisher, so I encouraged her to do so.

What I didn't know that day we looked through the old manuscripts was that my Aunt Dorothy was preparing for death and was putting her affairs in order. My encouragement sent her back to school, and she became one of the best kindergarten teachers God ever made. Encouragement works.

When I was 60 years old, I decided to become a writer; but the impetus had come at the age of 19 when I was at the University of Oregon, taking a course in creative writing. A professor chose my short story to read in front of the class. That bit of encouragement stuck with me for 41 years and played a large part in my decision to write. Encouragement is a powerful tool.

If at any time you are having difficulties with a loved one, try encouragement. Sometimes we take advantage of the ones we love and fall into the kind of nagging and carping that everyone—except the one doing it—recognizes as criticism. Instead, try speaking a word of praise and encouragement. You will be amazed at how influential you can be.

Prayer and Blessing

One of the most difficult passages in the Bible is the statement of Jesus, "Love your enemies, do good to those who hate you, bless those who curse you, pray for those who mistreat you" (Luke 6:27-28). These words are so contrary to our unregenerate nature, which loves those who love us and hates those who hate us, that they are rarely practiced. Whenever someone dares to follow them, however, the results are amazing.

One time a man threatened to kill me. He called the house over and over, spewing out his hate and venom. One day he threatened to use a gun.

I responded in anger. "Well, two can play that game. I can use a gun too."

His attacks increased in vigor. Then I decided to put this serious problem into God's hands. When the man called again, I said to him, "God bless you. I want you to know I am praying for you." That's the last time I heard from him.

When you are dealing with problem people, remember that prayer works. Instead of criticizing, try blessing the person you want to change. But then be prepared—because the one most likely to change is *you!*

In an episode of the once popular television series "Little House on the Prairie" (based on the series of books written by Laura Ingalls Wilder), the hero rescued a young woman from her cruel father, who had beaten her because she loved a village boy. In the process the father tipped over a lamp and burned the house down. The scene that impressed me showed the father condemning his daughter in a bitter, harsh, unforgiving spirit. The hero looked at him with sorrow and said, "I'll pray for you." Sometimes that's all we have. There are no answers but to turn the problem over to God.

Once I helped a family with their delinquent boy. Following my advice, the parents tried every loving, encouraging method I suggested. I taught them to toughen their love and provide a program of discipline for the young man. No matter what we did, the 16-year-old countered with hate every act of love and with rebellion every act of control. I remember the day the officers handcuffed him and took him to prison.

The mother sobbed and sobbed and cried helplessly, "What can we do now?"

I said to her, "All we have left is to love him, visit him, and pray for him. He is no longer in our hands." When someone is no longer in our hands, we must release him or her to a power greater than ours.

Several years later, the young man made peace with himself and society. Prayer and blessing do work.

Suppose other people are doing something you think

is not right, and you believe they need to change. The way that seems somewhat natural to the uninformed is to attack the person by criticizing and pointing out the error. Such a tactic often provokes a counterattack and ends with hurt feelings or worse. By contrast, God's way uses one of the most powerful devices for changing and motivating people—the power of prayer and blessing.

If you think a person is your enemy, walk up to him or her, open up your heart, put wings of grace on your tongue and say, "Bless you," or "God bless you," or "I give you my blessing." When you offer a blessing to a person, the chances of positive change are much greater than when you give the curse of criticism.

One woman was very angry at me because I had declared in court that she was not a fit mother. She did not see herself that way, but I could come to no other conclusion. She became my enemy for life. But I will continue to pray for her. If we ever come face to face again, no matter what harsh words she says to me, I intend to say to her, "May God richly bless you."

■ Summary

Instead of criticizing, consider these ideas:

1. *Love and accept others.*
   Don't expect people to conform to your way of doing things; accept their way sometimes.
2. *Teach what is right.*
   If you believe your method is correct, take time to teach others, and maybe both you and they will learn.
3. *Dialog.*
   Talk it over before you attack. Maybe you'll discover that the other person is right.

4. *Reward appropriate behavior.*
   Focus your attention on the good. Maybe the bad will disappear without attention.
5. *Correct errors, not people.*
   Don't make it necessary for people to defend their egos because of their mistakes.
6. *Encourage others.*
   Motivate them to do what is right by cheering them on. Good words inspire good deeds.
7. *Pray for people and bless them.*
   Animals snarl at their enemies. Christians work to change enemies to friends.

4
How to Correct Others Without Hurting Them

Sam literally stinks! His body odor causes people to shun him, and then he feels hurt. My problem is, shall I join the group of people who consider Sam an outcast, or should I try to help him? If I try to help him, somewhere, somehow, I will be compelled to tell him that he needs to bathe more often. But Sam already feels rejected, and he is defensive and angry. What should I do?

Sara is so dominant and aggressive, such a super-mother and superwife, that she is smothering her husband. As a result, he is beginning to drift away from her. Someone needs to tell Sara that men have a hard time being romantic with their "mothers." She needs to stop being so bossy or she will lose her husband. But I don't want to confront Sara because she blames everything on everyone else.

Mary is spoiling her five-year-old to such an extent that any time she comes to visit, people pull the blinds, lock the door, and hide under the bed. They do not want to cope with her five-year-old terror. Neither do they want to tell the 25-year-old mother that she is being dominated by her obnoxious child.

The major premise of this book is: "Criticism doesn't work." We need to find other methods to correct Sam, Sara, and Mary. The other techniques, however, require planning and great care. Sometimes, when a person is standing on the edge of a cliff, ready to fall off, the only thing that works is to say loudly and quickly, "Get away from the edge of that cliff!"

The best procedure in interpersonal relationships is not to criticize. And yet, sometimes, the cruelest thing we can do is to fail to tell someone that he or she is on a collision course with disaster.

In addition, sometimes we find that praise and encouragement do not motivate someone, and ignoring the negative behavior may not always extinguish it. Whether we like it or not, sometimes we are left with the task of being a critic. Criticism is an emergency technique to be used only when we do not have the time to use a better technique or when other techniques have failed.

If you feel you have no choice but to offer your criticism, or if you need to speak up because the situation has become intolerable, then here are some suggestions gleaned from a half-century of counseling that seem to take some sting from the whip of criticism.

Use criticism with care

First, it is important to realize that criticism is a weapon that may very well destroy sensitive people. Use it with extreme care. According to *The World Almanac,* approximately 30,000 people commit suicide in the United

States each year. Other sources include uncertain suicides and go as high as 150,000. Who can say how many do it because they have been too harshly criticized? Several research studies have strongly suggested that rejection and loss of self-esteem precede suicide. Rejection can be caused by harsh, critical words; and loss of self-esteem often results from criticism.

When King Saul heard the women sing the battle song, "Saul has slain his thousands, and David his tens of thousands," he became so incensed by this implied criticism that he went mad and spent the rest of his days chasing David with murderous intent (1 Samuel 18:7). Like King Saul, people can become extremely angry, hostile, or even violent when they are criticized. So be careful of what you may unleash when you criticize.

When you criticize others, do not reinforce your strong words with shouting or emotional force. Do not use sarcasm, innuendos, or hidden meanings. It is easy to get angry at the truth when it comes with emotional force, so criticize softly and gently. A soft, gentle, and straightforward statement like, "Dear, please don't put your dirty shoes on the clean rug," will get a better response than the same words said in a scream with tears of anguish.

Be sure you are not guilty of the same behavior you are criticizing

One of the strongest admonitions the New Testament contains are the words of Jesus: "Why do you look at the speck of sawdust in your brother's eye and pay no attention to the plank in your own eye? How can you say to your brother, 'Let me take the speck out of your eye,' when all the time there is a plank in your own eye? You hypocrite, first take the plank out of your own eye, and then you will see clearly to remove the speck from your brother's eye" (Matthew 7:3-5).

The apostle Paul repeated the warning of Jesus: "You, therefore, have no excuse, you who pass judgment on someone else, for at whatever point you judge the other, you are condemning yourself, because you who pass judgment do the same things" (Romans 2:1).

When we are guilty and accuse someone else of the wrong, we are trying to shift the blame. For a thief to call someone else a thief puts the thief in double jeopardy. He or she then becomes not only a thief but also a hypocrite. Much of the destructive criticism of this world could be eliminated if people would remember to work out their own problems first.

Point out the positive

A negative attitude can easily become habitual. To avoid this, make certain that anytime you criticize someone, you also point out the positive aspects of his or her behavior. In this way you can save yourself from becoming a critic and also soften the blow against the other person.

To say, "Barbara, you did not dust the dresser; I'm disappointed in you," and not notice that Barbara made the bed, vacuumed the floor, washed the curtains, and cleaned the windows, is not fair. Yet how often we fall into that trap. Whenever we must criticize, let us also be equally prompt to praise good behavior.

The television programs, newspapers, and magazines in our country do not present the world "as it is" but instead "how bad it is." Sometimes I think the emphasis on bad news in America will become a self-fulfilling prophecy. I do not believe we should ignore the negative, but neither do I believe that we should emphasize the negative to the point that we ignore the positive. Realistically and pragmatically, in criticizing people, we must consider both the positive and the negative. It would be well if our news media did the same.

Don't attack self-esteem

The Bible contains two basic truths—the law and the gospel. The law teaches us that God hates sin; the gospel teaches us that God loves sinners. God loves sinners and hates their sin. We would be wise to do the same. When you are correcting, it makes sense not to put people down, destroy their self-esteem, or attack their egos.

I wish my father had known about personhood and self-esteem. It took me 30 years to get over the way Dad criticized me. For example, one day I was chopping wood, and I hit the wood box with the ax. My father did not say, "Son, I appreciate your chopping wood for our fireplace, but axes are very dangerous, and you can easily get hurt. Can you imagine what would have happened if instead of missing the wood and hitting the wood box, you missed the wood and hit yourself? I love you, Son, so be careful."

My father did not criticize like that. What he said was, "You dumb jerk. What's wrong with you? Don't you have any brains?" Then he slapped me hard and said, "You fix that wood box today, or I'll beat the - - - - out of you."

My father practically destroyed my self-esteem and who I was as a person. I still have to struggle with what I heard from my father about myself. So now I tell other parents to criticize the sin when they must, but show grace to the sinner in order to preserve that person's sense of worth.

Learn the art of "I messages"

In learning to criticize other people without hurting them, psychologists have learned that there are several words we need to be very careful in using. These words are *you, must, shouldn't, always,* and *never. You* is an attack, *must* is a command, *should* is a guilt trip, and *always* and *never* are absolutes.

Instead of saying, "You are driving too fast," say, "I don't like fast driving." The word *I* is emphasized, rather than the personal word *you.* To say, "You are a liar," makes a personal attack that can end only in defensiveness and a counterattack. Instead, say, "My experience is different," or "I have a hard time seeing it that way," or "I'll have to think about that," or any combination of words that softens the direct attack of, "You're a liar."

When we criticize, we are not out to get a person; we are out to change a behavior. So if we say, "That is very upsetting to me," we change the emphasis from "you the liar" to "I am upset." When we keep personal accusations out of criticism and instead state *how* we feel about that person's behavior, we will save precious egos and increase the possibility of improving behavior.

To say, "You must go to church next Sunday," is a command that meets with automatic resistance from people who are striving to think for themselves and be independent. Rather, say, "We are having an excellent program at church next Sunday. Would you like to come?" The person might not come, but he or she will have trouble resisting you because the emphasis has been shifted from a command to an invitation.

When we say, "You shouldn't smoke cigarettes," we are projecting our value system and trying to place guilt on another person who probably has plenty of guilt already. Increasing guilt does not necessarily change behavior. Rather, it elicits the anger instinct that wants to fight back. If we say, "I am allergic to cigarette smoke," we shift the emphasis from "you shouldn't" to "I am" or "I feel"—from their defect to your problem.

If we say, "You are *always* late," we make the other person feel hopeless, as if there were no possibility of his or her ever being on time. If we say, "I feel anxious when you are late," we are talking about our problem and giving him or her a chance to alleviate our suffering. When other people are *always* anything, they feel like giving up.

When we say, "You never do anything right," we take away from the person any virtue, hope, and possibility of making things right. Perhaps we could say, "You didn't do that job right," or better still, "I felt that last job could use some improvement."

Some people will get angry at anything we say. When we learn the art of "I" messages and leave out attack words like *you, must, shouldn't, always,* and *never,* others are less likely to be offended.

Tell people how you feel, not what they did wrong

The difference between "I" messages and "you" messages has proven to be a practical and effective psychological principle. Instead of walking up to your friend Brad and saying, "You were wrong when you told Jane her dress was inappropriate," say instead, "Brad, I felt embarrassed when you told Jane her dress was inappropriate."

Between a husband and wife, it is particularly true that direct criticism will cause defensiveness, which usually leads to an argument. When a husband or wife says, "I feel hurt," or "I feel neglected," or "I feel rejected," or "I feel you don't love me," a response can be made to feelings rather than a direct attack. When a husband or wife says, "You hurt me or neglected me or rejected me," with an emphasis on the word *you,* it invites a critical response because it is criticism.

The act of criticizing is deceptive. Supervisors can cut employees to shreds with criticism and get them to do what they want, but their employees can hardly stop themselves from developing an attitude of quiet resistance. That's just the way human nature is—when people feel put down, they subconsciously resist those who have criticized them.

For example, Chuck is harshly told by Mr. Stoneman to contact each supplier within three days. Chuck will probably do it, but the way he does it may cost the business some accounts. It's hard to put your heart into what you're doing when your ego is bruised. Chuck subconsciously begins a program of passive resistance. If Mr. Stoneman had learned how to criticize others without hurting them, he would have gotten the job done much more efficiently.

When I tell those I work with and those I love how I *feel,* rather than what they did wrong, then I am more likely to get the desired results from them without creating a program of passive resistance in them.

Correct in love

The catalysts that make criticism particularly toxic are resentment and bitterness, so correct others in love. Sarcasm is not love. Putting people down is not love. Making another person the object of a cruel joke is not love. Rejecting a person with words is not love. Pointing out another person's failings in a derogatory way is not love.

Love is described so well in 1 Corinthians 13:

> Love is patient, love is kind. It does not envy, it does
> not boast, it is not proud. It is not rude, it is not self-
> seeking, it is not easily angered, it keeps no record of
> wrongs. Love does not delight in evil but rejoices with
> the truth. It always protects, always trusts, always
> hopes, always perseveres.

Because I know God loves me with this kind of love, I
am able to show this love to others.

Turn criticism into correction

Criticism can be replaced by a more positive action—
correction. Correction implies that something is wrong—if
we erase the wrong and put in the right, we have a correction.
Criticism is often a put-down, while correction is a "put-right."
Criticism is a destructive attack, while correction is teaching.
To tell someone what is wrong is often futile, but to help
someone correct a bad situation is an exercise in caring.

On an assembly line in an automobile plant, highly-
skilled engineers are assigned the task of quality control. It
is their job to correct any errors made in the assembly of an
automobile. The more quality control, the more valuable the
product. To stand back and *criticize* someone's work is
hurtful, but to *correct* errors is positive and valuable.

Don't just criticize—help

In *Some Fruits of Solitude,* William Penn said: "They
have a right to censure that have a heart to help." It is easy
to point out what the other person is doing wrong. It is
much more difficult to help make it right.

Teachers often ask young children to bring something

from home and explain what it is and what to do with it. Perhaps we need to remember this "show and tell" procedure. When you see someone doing something that you feel like criticizing, show and tell instead. Before you criticize what is wrong, *show* him or her how to do it and *tell* him or her how to do it.

Once I was working with a group of volunteers who were painting an old church. One man set himself up as the foreman to tell us all what to do. One young man threw a rope around the steeple and hoisted himself high off the ground to paint that difficult spot. With the paint bucket dangling from his belt buckle, he hung on to the rope with one hand and painted fast and furiously with the other. The foreman on the ground yelled up at him, "You're splattering paint. Slow down." The young man shinnied down the rope and handed the foreman the bucket and the brush, saying, "Show me how."

Whenever you find it necessary to open your mouth and point out other people's flaws, consider for a moment doing, helping, and showing. Their job may not be as easy as you think.

I once went on a camping trip with a group of people to the Baja peninsula. One man volunteered to cook with the following condition: "I will cook the meals. But if you do not like the food and you criticize it, then you're the cook." I remember thinking, "These beans could use more seasoning," but I said to myself, "I would much rather eat the beans I did not like than to be the cook and have other people criticize my food." Since I did not have the heart to help, I did not have the right to criticize.

Use the sandwich approach

Raw criticism can be compared to raw meat. Seldom

can we force even a hungry person to eat a hunk of raw meat. Raw meat must be made palatable by cooking it. Similarly, criticism must be thought over in order to "cook" the idea and make it more tender.

My favorite sandwich shop makes a sandwich by placing cooked meat between two pieces of freshly baked bread, then adding lettuce, tomatoes, and whatever other condiments the customer prefers. Fresh bread can be compared to sincere compliments. Lettuce and tomatoes and other condiments are like qualifying statements, what you think of to say to take the harshness out of the criticism.

The sandwich approach starts with fresh bread—compliments—to which we add the meat of thoughtful criticism, followed by the seasoning of careful wording. The carefully qualified meat of criticism has been tenderly prepared between easy-to-digest compliments.

Criticism must be done with great care to keep from hurting those we need to correct. Each criticism needs to be sandwiched between at least two compliments. Then, when you give your criticism, it has been cooked carefully in thought and tact, fully seasoned in the sauces of love, and surrounded by praise.

■ Summary

When we criticize and point the finger of shame and blame, we need to be sure we are not guilty of the same thing.

We also need to point out the positive. We all need self-esteem. To attack the person destroys self-esteem; to help him or her improve raises it.

We can learn the art of giving "I" messages rather than the attacks of "you shouldn't." To tell people how we feel rather than what they did wrong builds bridges instead of walls.

If we must criticize, we should try to do it from a heart of love with the idea of "putting right" rather than "putting down."

We can remember how cheap it is to criticize people who actually need help. Instead of saying something *against* them, do something *for* them.

I suppose many people are harshly critical because they think things should be as *they* think they should be. Thomas Á Kempis, in *The Imitation of Christ,* said, "Be not angry that you cannot make others as you wish them to be, since you cannot make yourself as you wish to be." Our words of criticism probably won't change anyone and may even make this world a worse place in which to live. If we truly want to change people, praise, rather than criticism, is the answer.

5

When You Are Your Own Self-Critic

I am a person with a disability. The trauma of polio at the age of five created in me a lifelong problem of feelings of rejection and inferiority. I am completely familiar with the use of braces, crutches, and wheelchairs.

As a child, I spent seven years in and out of orthopedic hospitals, having a total of 13 surgeries. For as long as I can remember I have struggled to keep myself mobile. Many times my hero was Franklin Delano Roosevelt, but sometimes I also identified with Quasimodo, the hunchback of Notre Dame. My legs are so deformed that no matter how much I build up my ego, it seems to crumble under the curious stares of those I meet on the beaches and streets of life.

When I grew up and became a minister, I always felt self-conscious about my exaggerated limp, though for the most part church members were very kind. I often wondered if I were "good enough" for the ministry.

Even now, as a professional clinical psychologist, I have

difficulty not being a professional self-critic. My body often refuses to do what I ask it to do. I work hard to keep myself from self-condemnation.

Everyone is disabled in some respect, and braces on the legs are different only in degree from braces on the teeth. Besides that, the greatest handicaps of all are not those in the body but those of the mind. And who can possibly be so arrogant as to think they are not mentally disabled in some way?

I've lived most of my life with a disability that everyone who meets me instantly notices. I have learned that the more I think about it, the more I talk about it, and the more I act like a disabled person, the more I become one. When I am performing at a high level, I do not think about my difficulties but about the work I have to do. I do not dwell on my insufficiencies but rather on what I have to offer. When I look at my defects and berate myself, the defects grow, and my self-esteem diminishes. When I look at my virtues and praise God, my defects disappear and my self-esteem becomes that of a child of God.

God loves us sinful human beings and wants us to love him. I can't love God and constantly criticize myself. If I criticize myself, it's as if I were criticizing God, who made me. How can I criticize someone who is so loved by Jesus that he gave his life to die for me?

God is sovereign over the kingdom of praise. Satan is prince over the world of criticism. The temptation is to think that even if we have to moderate our criticism of other people in order to preserve their lives, we do not have to moderate our criticism of ourselves. Too many people believe the false idea that it is a godlike, proper thing to continually criticize oneself.

When people criticize themselves, they become their own enemies. Consequently, they often turn off their immune system, weaken their autonomic nervous system, and destroy their ability to function properly, which makes it difficult for them to relate to other people.

When people succumb to the temptation to call themselves dumb, stupid, or incompetent, they actually help bring these qualities about. What you say and think about yourself you will become.

A 20-year-old man once told me how much he longed to leave home and become independent, but he felt unable to work, unable to go to school, and unable to leave his parents' house. He said, "All my life I never could do anything good enough to please my parents, and now I can't do anything to please myself. I always have been a nerd, and I always will be one." He sighed and bowed his head in deep depression. His parents' critical attitude had become his own.

The self-critic is self-destructive. When we discover our failings, we can ask God for forgiveness and try to do better. If we criticize ourselves for our failings, we erode our motivation to improve.

I'm not, however, recommending that people go around breaking their arms by patting themselves on the back. Neither am I recommending a constant flow of bragging words. Such conduct makes a person seem to be an arrogant loudmouth. One cannot prove one's worth by saying, "I am the greatest."

The following suggestions grow out of my own experience in dealing with my self-criticism and the ideas I pass on to people who are being destroyed by their own self-criticism.

Never recognize one of your failings without recognizing a virtue

It is easy to get into the habit of overlooking the good things you do and overresponding to the bad things. Never criticize yourself and let it stand alone. This conditions the mind, particularly the primitive brain stem, to turn against itself. The unconscious mind can be programmed to be an enemy to the conscious mind. Then, when the conscious mind sets itself on some achievement, the unconscious mind, as a deep-seated enemy, scuttles the program.

To keep from becoming a loser, become your own friend. To do this, remind yourself of your virtues. I am not saying, "Don't recognize your faults." I am merely saying, "Be fair, and recognize your virtues too."

A medical professional had experienced a number of devastating defeats and had been treating a group of neurotic complainers. One day all the negativism caught up with her, and she became very ill. According to her, everything had gone wrong, nothing worked anymore, and she could not think of a single thing she had done right. Over and over again she repeated, "I'm no good; I can't do anything right." It took a long time and much support and encouragement to win that person back from the valley of the shadow of depression. She had to learn to focus on her strengths and accomplishments.

Give yourself praise and rewards

When a person does something wrong, he or she often gets punished. When a person does something right, he or she is often ignored. In a perverse way, such a procedure encourages wrong behavior because that is what gets attention. We all need to improve our behavior. And when the slightest improvement is shown, we need to give ourselves a pat on the head in order to keep the improvements coming.

Behavior modification is a proven, scientific process of working with children. It is based on a reward system that considers what children want and then gives them a portion of what they want when they do what is desired. Simply stated, recognize and reward good behavior.

Most of the shaping and most of the encouraging that we get in this world come not from other people, but from ourselves. If we fail to praise ourselves and give ourselves rewards when we do the right thing, our behavior will probably not improve.

Whisper your wrongs, shout your rights

Practice a soft, kind tone when you tell yourself that you have done something wrong. Use a loud, vigorous, enthusiastic voice when talking about the things you do right. If you lose a race because you stumble, shrug your shoulders slightly and say with a wry grin, "I goofed," or "I lost." When you win a race, jump up and down, rejoice, and congratulate yourself. Allow yourself to be pleased with yourself.

We are sometimes told that praising is arrogant and shouting a loud "hurrah" when we win is rude. Not so. I have deliberately practiced both self-praise and loud congratulations as a cure for my inferiority complex. I have never yet been censured; in fact, people are delighted when I win and shout loudly about my victory. When we criticize ourselves for every mistake and shrug off every winning move, life becomes drudgery, and we become so surly that no one wants us around. Whisper your wrongs and shout your victories, and others will want such a positive, enthusiastic winner as their friend.

Accept compliments graciously

Never respond to a compliment by saying, "It was nothing." If you are wearing your oldest dress and someone says, "What a pretty outfit," do not respond by saying, "This old rag? I got it at the thrift store ten years ago." It is not wise to question people's judgment or put down their complimentary remarks. When we encourage other people to speak nicely about us, we will be more likely to do so too.

Once I met a self-effacing, negative woman with a huge inferiority complex. She allowed everyone to take advantage of her; no one liked her, and she hated herself. One day I said to her, "That was the best cake I have ever eaten. You are a wonderful cook."

She replied with a pitifully self-critical tone, "It wasn't any good. You're only saying that to try to make me feel good. I never do anything right."

I decided right there that I would enter into a campaign to change that woman. So I said in a very harsh voice, "You have insulted me. I know a good cake when I taste one, and I resent your questioning my judgment."

She took a long time to change, but now she has many friends and is no longer self-effacing. She learned one simple lesson: accept compliments graciously.

When someone gives you a compliment, do not ignore it or fend it away or say, "Oh, it wasn't anything." Look the person in the eye, smile broadly, and say, "Thank you, I'm glad you liked it." Or say, "I did the best I could. I'm happy you appreciated it."

Look at the positive side

In the process of looking on the positive side of life, do not neglect to look on the positive side of you. We know more about ourselves than anyone else. We know about our secret failings, but we also know the good things we have done. We encourage the good in ourselves by paying attention to our positive achievements and minimizing our failures.

Betty always thought everyone else was wonderful and life was a beautiful place. But in her childhood she had somehow gained the self-defeating habit of looking on the negative side of herself. Betty was a textbook case of "You're okay; I'm not okay." Perhaps she expected to win friends and influence people by telling everyone how wonderful they were. Or perhaps she expected to garner gold stars in her crown by being so humble. In any case, Betty was ill for the simple reason that she despised herself.

One day she said, "Oh, Dr. Diehm, you are so wonderful. I wish I could be like you. Everything I do is wrong. I feel so sick."

"No wonder you feel that way, Betty," I replied. "Isn't there any way you can see some virtue in yourself? Look at how well-dressed you are. Look at what fine meals you prepare."

Betty recognized many positive things around her, but she needed help in seeing what was positive about herself and her life.

Be your own cheerleader

You can encourage yourself with such words as, "You can do it. Come on, friend, I'm proud of you." Treat yourself as if you were a fragile, sensitive, little child with an inferiority complex. Be extremely careful of what you say to that fragile child. If the child believes your cruel words, he or she will only get worse. Cheer yourself on with constant words of encouragement and praise.

Most of us remember the children's story about the little engine that could. "I think I can, I think I can, I think I can" is what it said when it climbed the hills of life. "I thought I could, I thought I could, I thought I could" is what it proudly puffed when it steamed into the station.

"I can do it, I can do it, I can do it" are the words we can teach our children as they tackle the tasks of life. And they are words we can speak to the child within ourselves.

Accept God's grace and forget the past

In your relationship to God, do not think of yourself as "such a worm as I." You are God's friend (John 15:15)—that's a very important person. You are God's child (Romans 8:16)—that means you belong to the family. Be proud of your relationship to the King of kings and Lord of lords. You can say, "Father, I have sinned," but then accept his forgiveness and forget about your sin.

The Bible portrays God's great anger at the griping and complaints of the children of Israel. Moses had all he could do to keep God from destroying the critics and starting over again. God doesn't like criticism; he likes praise. So God certainly does not like it when people constantly berate themselves. If you must call your sins to God's attention, then accept God's forgiveness and concentrate on what you have done well this day.

■ Summary

Criticism is as dangerous as a surgeon's knife in the hands of a madman. The surgeon's knife in the hands of a trained, intelligent professional cuts out bad tissue and is used with care not to damage the good cells. It is extremely rare for surgeons to operate on themselves.

Self-criticism should be as rare as self-surgery.

Change yourself by praise, rewards, and friendly encouragement. More than anything else, change yourself by recognizing that we are motivated not by God's law or by God's judgment, but by God's love and grace. Knowing that God loves you sets you free to love yourself. When you believe God is pleased with you and your accomplishments, you can praise and reward yourself—and that opens the way to further positive change.

Part Two:
Receiving Criticism

1. What did you learn?
impression that God doesn't
want to hear us complain
  p. 69

"Criticism can be avoided only
by saying nothing, doing nothing,
and being nothing." p. 70

6

Coping with Criticism

We have been talking about giving criticism—how to moderate our speech so the other person will not be hurt by our words of correction. Now we enter into a shift of emphasis—how to cope with criticism. We cannot stop other people from criticizing us, so we need to learn how to receive criticism.

During the Korean War, when Chinese troops captured large numbers of American soldiers, the Chinese incarcerated them in prison camps, where they were isolated and criticized. When these men were separated from their officers and received no support, they often developed serious psychological problems that sometimes led to death.

When Pat Brown was governor of California, he gave Caryl Chessman, a prisoner on death row, a 60-day stay of execution. Many people were so angry at this that they booed Governor Brown wherever he went. In 1962 Brown faced a re-election campaign against then former Vice-President

Richard Nixon, whom he was able to defeat. But Brown declared, "When the crowd cheered Richard Nixon and booed me in front of my wife and daughter, I experienced the greatest hurt of my life."

In the course of life we need to learn how to cope with criticism from wherever it comes and for whatever reason it is given. Some people respond to criticism by withdrawing into an inner shell of silence and hurt. Others overrespond with a battery of verbal defense mechanisms. The silent response ends in inner, repressed hurt. The verbal response ends in a war of angry words. Both silence and verbal counterattack tend to destroy relationships.

When we are on the receiving end of criticism, here are some suggestions to help us deal with it.

Examine your anger

If criticism makes you too angry, stop and think. If the criticism is justified and is spoken in love, why should you be angry? If the criticism is unfair and bitter, again, why should you be angry? If you get angry, you don't have any strength to deal with the critics. If the criticism is justified, respond in gratitude. If the criticism is unfair, respond in good humor. When you become angry and defensive, you may harm those who are trying to help you. Then you may become even more bitter.

Few people bother to understand their weaknesses until they are in such serious trouble that there seems no solution. Be grateful that the critic, whether justified or unjustified, has called your attention to a weakness. Thank the critic and begin a program to correct your weakness.

When people criticize, it is helpful to recognize the possibility of your angry response and to be prepared to control

1. Withdraw
2. Over respond with verbal defense

it. It helps me to ask God to help me. Every morning before I face the critics of the day, I pray something like this:

> Dear Lord,
>   Soon I will be doing the work I think you want me to do. Some people will tell me what I am doing is wrong. Help me not be distracted by them and keep my mind fixed upon my goal.
> Amen.

Another way of coping with our angry response to criticism is *sublimation.* With the help of God, we can use our anger to boost ourselves to higher planes of achievement. Control yourself, and try not to allow the critics to make you angry. If they do, use the anger to complete your work, not to fight your critics.

One day a middle-aged man came to see me and said, "My father hooks me. Every time he talks to me, he makes me angry. Every word he says seems to be critical. I am so angry that I can't do my work."

I said to him, "Now that you know your father's critical words make you angry, you can help him and yourself by planning your response. Before your father can say a word, say to him, 'Thank you, Dad, for your words of criticism that help me to improve myself.' "

To cope with criticism, we need to become aware of what makes us angry and take steps to ward off confrontations. I am pleased to report that my angry friend's words of appreciation were able to soften his father's criticism.

Respond slowly

Criticism is a sharp, hot sword that pierces swiftly. If we respond quickly, our movement will cause the sword to go deeper. Furthermore, as we lash back defensively, we are also likely to hit the other person with our own sword and do irreparable damage.

When someone attacks us with criticism, instead of stabbing back, we need to put up the shield of self-control. We should not respond quickly, because instantaneous responses are almost always wrong.

When I am criticized, I try to respond slowly. I think about the criticism prayerfully, and decide whether it is a weapon or a surgeon's knife. If it is a surgeon's knife, I allow it to cut out what needs to be cut out. If it is a street fighter's uncontrolled knife of vengeance, I neutralize it in my mind by not giving it back.

It takes a long time to build, but it is easy to destroy. Remember that critics are taking the quick way. Slow them down by not responding too quickly.

Respond gently

One day a brush salesman rang the doorbell at a woman's home. He started to tell her the advantages of owning his company's brushes. Instead of saying, "No, thank you, I have all the brushes I need," she swore at him and slammed the door. The man rang the doorbell again. When she angrily opened the door, he exclaimed, "I am so sorry if I said anything to offend you. I would much rather have your good will than sell you a brush. Please tell me what it was I said that made you so angry, because I don't want to say that any more."

The woman softened and said, "I've just been having a bad day. I'm sorry I slammed the door." Then she bought a brush.

Just as that woman transferred her anger from the bad

day to the salesman, so people often transfer their unhappiness onto us. When people criticize you, don't stomp off angrily, but be gentle. Perhaps you will sell a brush, and even more important, perhaps you will calm an angry critic.

One day a couple who were on the verge of a divorce came to see me. They quarreled constantly about everything. Neither felt he or she could do anything to please the other. I said to the woman, "You are so intense that every word you say is like a shout. Be gentle. Speak softly. Even when your words are not critical, your tone makes them sound critical."

This particular woman was open to suggestions for improvement. She said to me, "You're right. I'll try to do that." She did try, and that helped their relationship considerably.

Strengthen your purpose

Some people are driven hard in every direction. They are lost on the high seas without a compass. They have lots of gas for their boat but no place to go.

Purpose for living is a compass, a direction, a goal. Meaning in life takes away the sting of the critic. Therefore, when you are criticized, respond by strengthening your goals, aims, and aspirations. Let the voice of the critic renew your purpose for living.

During World War II, psychiatrist Viktor Frankl learned a valuable lesson in a Nazi concentration camp. Those people in the camps who had goals and purpose also had meaning in their lives and were frequently able to survive. The same thing is true of the many people today who are rejected and criticized for being different. A person can survive almost any insult if life has direction and meaning.

When my children graduated from high school, I insisted

that they choose a direction. Since I paid for it, I did not allow them to go to college without deciding what they wanted to be. They could change later in life, for changing direction is often necessary. But to wander endlessly, never knowing where one wants to go or what one wants to be, makes a person vulnerable, particularly to rejection. Lack of purpose makes us weak, and a weak person can easily be destroyed by words of criticism. Purpose makes us strong.

Let criticism give you a loving heart

People who are angry and hateful often respond to critics with such explosive energy that they self-destruct. If we care for people, we can listen to them, and when they shoot angry darts at us, we can make allowances. Do not allow your critics to make you into a critic. Instead, let their sharp words call forth a loving response.

Being a peacemaker is not easy. In fact, it is so difficult to respond lovingly to anger that the Bible qualifies the command to live at peace with everyone with the words, "If it is possible, as far as it depends on you" (Romans 12:18). Only God's Spirit working within us can make that possible.

The stimuli of life are frequently beyond our control. We seldom choose whether it's going to rain or how Jane Doe is going to talk to us. Our response is under our control, and we can say, "Oh, rats, it's raining!" or "Hurrah, what a beautiful rain!" We can respond to Jane Doe's rudeness with another rude remark, or we can assume a loving heart and be sweet to the person who is sour. If we determine in advance and set our mind to it, we can let criticism be a trigger to set off words of appreciation.

In Matthew 5:39, Jesus said, "If someone strikes you on the right cheek, turn to him the other also. " As I have grown older, I have realized that statement could be paraphrased, "When people attack you with bitter, critical words that feel like a slap in the face, do not respond in kind. Rather, overcome their cruel words by good ones of your own." Christians have often debated whether it works to turn the other cheek physically, but I do know that it is an effective tactic to overcome critical words in a verbal battle.

Realize you could be wrong

A person who is puffed up with pride is vulnerable to the pinpricks of criticism. In fact, the prideful person invites criticism, just as the rude person who pushes in front of you and then leans over invites a kick in the pants.

Anyone can be wrong, and everyone is wrong sometimes. Those people who have difficulty admitting they are wrong develop strong defensive techniques to protect themselves and are very vulnerable to criticism, usually responding in an angry way to anyone who dares to give them a suggestion. Such an attitude will bring to that person more than the usual number of antagonists.

In the Sermon on the Mount Jesus said, "Blessed are the poor in spirit, for theirs is the kingdom of heaven" (Matthew 5:3). The poor in spirit are those who recognize they need help. They haven't arrived yet. They realize they could be wrong. One of the signs of emotional health is the ability to accept correction.

Speak pleasantly

It is impossible to avoid the critics; they are everywhere. But being pleasant makes it easier to endure their thrusts, and a pleasant response is the best way to stop further criticism.

I am thinking of two men who came to see me for psychotherapy. The first man had trouble controlling his anger. He had estranged his wife and children, divided his church, and generally made life difficult for those around him. He had adopted the view that he had to talk exactly according to the way he felt. He felt angry, so he thought he had to talk angrily.

By contrast, I counseled another young man who had the same problem, yet he had such a pleasant disposition that, like Joseph of old, even the judges and jailers loved him.

Both men had the same psychological problem. The first man had a constant swarm of enemies. The second man had a constant collection of friends. The friends constantly tried to defend his bad actions, whereas the unpleasant fellow had people trying to destroy him.

When we speak unpleasantly, we invite criticism as surely as a snarling dog invites attack. When we speak pleasantly, we screen ourselves from much criticism.

Consider criticism a motivator

Criticism can easily make us bitter or just as easily make us sweet. Our attitude can be, "How nice it is for these people to take the time to tell me what I ought to do." Criticism can be a club to knock us down, or a prod to drive us forward. Many persons have become great trying to prove to their critics that they could do what critics said they could not do.

Demosthenes listened to the critics make fun of him, and he stuffed his mouth with pebbles to practice speaking until he became one of the world's greatest orators. As a boy, Teddy Roosevelt was laughed at and called "four eyes" and "sissy." It so motivated him that he became president of the United States. Life provides many challenging stories of those who have overcome their critics. How can we become one of those winners? The answer is found in our determination that criticism will not put us down but drive us up.

Talk to God about it

One of the best ways to express your frustration with your critics is to bring it to God in prayer. Throughout the Bible there are examples of men and women who suffered unjustly from the criticism and derision of those around them, people who brought these concerns to God. The figure of Job, who unjustly suffered and complained about it to God, is a good example. Many of the psalms reflect the psalmist's anger and frustration in the form of prayer.

Many people are under the impression that God wants to hear only nice things from us and doesn't want to hear us complain. Nothing could be farther from the truth. God wants us to be open and honest with him about our problems and concerns. Bringing our anger to God in prayer avoids the problems of lashing out at our friends or critics and can be a constructive way of dealing with it.

Praise the Lord

Merlin R. Carothers, U.S. Army Chaplain, served in Viet Nam. After release, he pastored a church in Escondido, California, and authored a series of books on praise. He hit upon a method to help people handle their troubles in bad times. I found his method also works for those who are trying to cope with criticism. Carothers suggested that people accept their problems and praise the Lord for everything. Since God is looking after us, all things work together for good. Troubles become blessings in disguise when we look at them through the eyes of faith.

I don't believe that any one thing works for everyone, but it does work for me to be grateful to God for all my *blessings*. When the pain of the critic's attack abates a little, thanking God and looking for the good in the bad words is an excellent exercise.

When someone has put you down and it hurts, when you feel the angry pain of the sting of criticism, stop for a moment, bow your head, and thank God for all the good things he has given to you. Before you enter into a war of words with the devil who is trying to take away what you have by overemphasizing what you don't have, praise the Lord for what you do have.

▉ Summary

In planning for the future, we must be very careful that we do not plan for opposition. To anticipate evil can bring a self-fulfilling prophecy. When people become suspicious of everyone, their very suspicion becomes their chief enemy. Though we do not plan opposition, we need not be surprised when it comes. Criticism can be avoided only by saying nothing, doing nothing, and being nothing.

When criticism comes your way, ask yourself why this criticism makes you angry and defensive. Then, respond slowly and gently, strengthen your purpose, let criticism give you a loving heart, realize you could be wrong, speak pleasantly, consider criticism a motivator, and most importantly, praise the Lord.

7
What to Do When Criticism Is Justified

Whether we like it or not, people do criticize us, sometimes very sharply. And, whether we like it or not, the most skillful users of behavior modification find that sometimes even they must call attention to what is wrong. When a person starts to jump over a cliff, there is no time to develop a reward system—our job is to get the person away from that cliff.

When criticism comes, as it must to all of us, there are a few questions we need to ask: Is this criticism justified? Is it all that important? What shall my response be?

If the criticism is delivered with a reasonable amount of sincerity, and you think the charge is true, instead of rejecting it or defending against it or counterattacking, there are a number of things you can do to profit from the criticism.

Be receptive to the truth

The Bible declares that David was a man after God's

own heart; yet it also tells of many things David did to displease God. David had an affair with Bathsheba and then had her husband Uriah killed. The prophet Nathan confronted David with a story about a rich man with flocks of sheep who had stolen the only pet sheep of a poor man. In anger David shouted, "As surely as the Lord lives, the man who did this deserves to die!" (2 Samuel 12:5).

The prophet then pointed his finger at King David, saying, "You are the man!"

Nathan was right, and David was wrong—and David admitted it. In this way he set a pattern for us. When we are wrong, we are to admit it quickly and definitely, and then begin the process of repentance and restitution.

It is possible that our critics are speaking the truth. If we respond by becoming defensive, we may be screening out a message from God. It is difficult to accept a critical word, but it is imperative that we search for truth and receive it from wherever it comes. The most profoundly effective criticism I ever received was from a girl in the first grade who told me in a guileless way what no one else dared to speak. I will be eternally grateful.

Confess your sin and take the consequences

When you are criticized, and the criticism is justified, it is best to confess and face it. To lie or defend or counter-attack only delays the inevitable. To proclaim your innocence in order to avoid or delay punishment succeeds only in prolonging the agony and making the punishment inevitably worse. If your critic is right, say crisply, "You are right. I am wrong. I will change. Thank you for calling it to my attention."

During my prison ministry, I had a group of inmates who

practiced therapy by using painful confrontations. Every new member of the group was asked why he was sentenced to prison. When the man explained, one of the inmates would reply, "And of course, you're innocent!" It became a standing joke, for we all realized that until a man could confess his guilt, he could not successfully receive help.

Confessing our sins is usually beneficial, but sometimes our confession of sin hurts other people. When I was a pastor, a man confessed publicly to immorality with another church member. You can't imagine what anguish that confession brought in our church. Some people in the congregation never recovered from it. I learned the hard way never to recommend public confession if that confession will damage someone else. If you are ever in that dilemma, I suggest you pray diligently and think carefully before you clear your conscience by harming someone else.

Express appreciation to the critic

No matter how difficult it is, we need to listen to criticism. Criticism can keep us from becoming too arrogant. We need to listen to the truth about ourselves so we can grow to be useful persons on the face of the earth.

Catch your critic off guard by giving him or her some praise. When you thank your critic, you do two things: you make yourself receptive to truth, and you soften the critic's blow.

One day a young man said to me, "Every time my mother tells me what to do or criticizes me for doing what I do, I find myself doing the opposite. I become so angry I can't control myself. What should I do?"

I thought long and hard about this problem because I struggle with the same resistance to correction from loved ones. I suggested to the young man that he respond to his mother's criticism with a quick, "Thank you." When his mother said a critical word like, "Son, you're staying out too late at night. You won't be in any condition to go to work, and I worry about you," he could say something like, "Thank you for the suggestion. I'll think it over, and maybe I can make a change."

Two weeks later I asked the young man, "How did my suggestion work?"

He responded, "It's a terrible suggestion. I hate it. I resist it with all my strength, and yet I have to admit it works. I find my mother's nagging becomes bearable when I say, 'Thank you for your suggestion.'"

We can learn to respond in kindness rather than in kind, to overcome evil with good, to not allow another person to set our standards. When anyone criticizes you, instead of automatic anger and defensiveness, try this statement: "Thank you for your suggestion. I'll think about it, and maybe I can change."

If we can change, we do change

Let us suppose we have been criticized and we realize the criticism is justified. We have made some allowance for our own feelings of inferiority, but still the critic has pointed out something we cannot deny. We then need to plan to make a change.

I was once criticized for making a racial remark. Up to that time, I had not considered myself to be a person who was prejudiced. I told the man who criticized me, "I can't see anything wrong with that remark."

He responded, "It may not be wrong to you, but it is offensive to the race you are talking about."

I decided he was right, and I never made that remark again. Criticism may embarrass or hurt us, but it can also be used to help us improve.

Change or refrain

Sometimes our critics are right but are talking about a personality characteristic or a slip of the tongue or some habit that is so ingrained that we cannot change. Some people's personalities are just naturally flamboyant, verbal, and dominant. Other people are more shy and prefer to be cooperative followers. To fault a shy person for not being bold may state truth, but it is unlikely that the person so criticized can do anything about it.

Do not let such critics turn you into a bitter, vengeful, malicious skeptic. The person who is bitter at injustice is the person most likely to perpetuate injustice. Bitterness becomes an angry substitute for justice. A person who is bitter at the government will not try to change the government, only destroy it.

Abraham Lincoln once wrote a sharp letter of reproof to General Mead for failing to attack General Lee when the situation was favorable. He said, "I do not understand, General, how you could have failed to attack General Lee when he was on your side of the river. Now that he is on the other side of the river, it is much more hazardous to attack. You have prolonged the war and cost us the lives of thousands of young men. I am deeply disappointed."

President Lincoln never mailed the letter. It was found among his papers after his death. Even though the criticism was justified, Lincoln may not have wanted to be guilty of bitterness, and so he criticized with reluctance. Perhaps no man in history has received more criticism than Abraham

Lincoln. His response to his critics was that he was doing the best he could. And when it was his turn to criticize, he would not allow even a hint of bitterness to creep in.

Plan a program of self-improvement

Perhaps the best suggestion for handling criticism is a positive one: plan your own program of self-improvement, and you will usually work out your weaknesses before the critics can get to you.

A well-known bumper sticker says, "Please be patient, God isn't finished with me yet." God works with us through a program of teaching and correction. In order to be taught and corrected, we must obey the biblical suggestion, "Do your best to present yourself to God as one approved, a workman who does not need to be ashamed and who correctly handles the word of truth" (2 Timothy 2:15). When we are diligent in a program of self-improvement, the critics have little to say.

At 6:00 every morning, the alarm goes off and I reach for my Bible. I read a minimum of three chapters a day. On Sundays I read ten or more. I systematically say my prayers, following a list of requests I write down. When I write down the requests, I can check on how often my prayers are answered. I also study a little psychology every day. I keep a list of jokes, poems, and favorite sayings. I look up one new word every day in the dictionary, and I spend one hour a day in secular reading, including the newspaper and certain magazines.

My routine may not work for anyone else, but we all can profit by disciplining ourselves, learning something every day, and having a program of goals toward which we are working.

Keep a list of your credits

Some people remember every good thing that has happened to them and forget life's evil events. Other people are more like me and find it easy to remember life's traumas, emphasizing the negative. One day I preached what I thought was a fairly good sermon. The congregation was appreciative, and 300 people filed out the front door, shaking my hand and congratulating me, saying, "Fine sermon this morning, Pastor." One disgruntled listener pointed out several inconsistencies, a mispronounced word, and some deficient reasoning.

Instead of thinking about the 300 people who thought my sermon was great, I focused on the criticism. I was so dismayed by the accuracy of the critic that I almost lost heart for my job. So I developed a protection against those who emphasize the negative: I started keeping a file of complimentary letters. I also started writing down some of the good things I have said and done. Whenever I feel discouraged by critics, I take the time to read those letters and my record of accomplishments.

I recommend to those people who have trouble receiving criticism that they keep a file of complimentary remarks and write down somewhere a list of the good things they have done. Prepare for the inevitable criticism that comes to us all, and keep a list of your appreciations to counter the depreciations.

Laugh at yourself

Television networks sometimes show a program that deals with the bloopers made by professional actors. Every time someone mispronounced a word, blew a line, or made some other error with the cameras running, the blooper became grist for the mill of the blooper show. I have never yet seen an actor or professional speaker who made a mistake and then engaged in self-criticism. Instead, they laugh and start over. Far from being embarrassed by the actors' bloopers, some directors show them at the end of a program while the credits are running.

So you make a blooper. When you notice it yourself, it is a little easier to laugh. When someone calls it to your attention and you haven't noticed it before, it's a little harder. But laughter is a better response to criticism than cursing, counterattack, or defensiveness. One of the best ways to take the angry sting out of the truthful critic is to throw back your head, laugh, and say, "I do that. I try not to. It gets the better of me. Thanks for calling it to my attention."

▇ Summary

So you are being criticized. What's more, your critic is right and you are wrong. What can you do? Be receptive to the truth, express appreciation to the critic, correct your error if possible, refrain from bitterness, plan your own program of self-improvement, keep a list of your credits, and be ready to laugh at yourself.

8

What to Do When Criticism Is Unfair

Some criticism is blatantly unfair and needs to be completely ignored, but most criticism has a grain of truth in it. Few political candidates have difficulty obtaining delicious tidbits of negative information about their opponents.

Many thousands of years ago, when Artaxerxes was king of Babylon, he sent his cupbearer, Nehemiah, back to Jerusalem to rebuild the walls of the city. Nehemiah worked hard at his task, but he had some enemies by the name of Sanballat, Tobiah, and Geshem. They did not want Nehemiah to build the wall, and they criticized him, listing every reason why he should not do it and why what he was doing was wrong. They decided to hold a conference and embarrass him by criticizing his behavior in front of the Jewish people. They tried to get him to meet in a village in the plain of Ono. Nehemiah sent a messenger to them saying, "I am carrying on a great project and cannot go down" (Nehemiah 6:3).

The attitude of Nehemiah is exactly the way we need to treat critics who try to stop what we are doing with their critical words and half-truths. Like Nehemiah, we involve ourselves in our work and refuse to come down to the level of critical faultfinding.

The road of life has many stumbling blocks. Among the most severe are the sharp, jagged stones of the critic. We need to decide whether we are going to stumble and fall at the first words of a critic or whether we will allow that stumbling block to become a stepping stone.

No one is free from the attacks of those who falsely accuse or who fill their accusations with just enough truth to make one stop and think. We need a method of dealing with these obstructions.

Keep unjustified criticism in perspective

Allow criticism to correct you, but not direct you. Choose your own direction. Rather, be directed by God, who usually lets you direct yourself. In any case, do not allow yourself to be directed by critics.

John Henry Newman, an English writer and church official, said: "Nothing would be done at all, if a man waited till he could do it so well that no one could find fault with it."

You do not have to respond to every ill-chosen word. Neither do you have to change your life direction because someone does not like the way you are going. Accept some correction from trusted friends and colleagues, but choose your own direction.

One day a man and his friend walked into a convenience store for a snack. The cashier was harsh, negative, and critical. The friend said to the man, "How can you possibly be pleasant to such a rude person?"

The man responded, "I will not allow a discourteous cashier to ruin my day. I—not my critics—will decide whether I am pleasant or unpleasant."

Receive criticism as a disguised compliment

Dale Carnegie taught that the best way to handle false or inaccurate criticism was to consider it a disguised compliment. He said, "No one ever kicks a dead dog. You have to be someone of importance in order to be criticized." So when people report something about you that is not true or is inaccurate, consider yourself so important that you have enemies taking a whack at you. Thieves do not steal from a man who has nothing, nor do people assassinate the character of a criminal. When you are criticized, let it boost your self-esteem.

In the story about the bird man of Alcatraz, there is a confrontation between the bird man and one of his enemies who appeared against him at every parole hearing. One day the bird man turned to his enemy and said, "You think you are something, but without me you are nothing. You get your greatness through your critical attacks that prevent me from being paroled."

The bird man was right. Some people's only claim to fame is their cowardly ability to throw rocks at public figures who live in glass houses. If someone is throwing rocks at you, consider yourself to be quite important.

Avoid giving people "bugging privileges"

Not long ago there was a noisy accident in front of our home. A teenaged driver with a carload of friends went roaring down the street and just missed our neighbor who was sweeping the curb. He retaliated in anger, threw a pop bottle after the racing car, and hit the rear window. The girl driving the car slammed on her brakes, put her car in reverse, and backed up for a confrontation. Some other teenagers in a van had been pursuing the girl. The car and the van collided with an ear-splitting crash. No one was hurt, but the teenagers in both cars jumped out of their vehicles and threatened the neighbor with loud, obscene language.

After the donnybrook subsided, the teenagers roared away before the police came. My neighbor who threw the bottle was quiet and subdued, sorry he had done such a foolish thing, and wallowing in hurt feelings from the insults of the teenagers.

I told him, "You can't afford to let everyone in the world have bugging privileges." Some things are not worth bringing into our system for a reaction.

Every day we all screen out things we do not want to experience. Sensors in the cerebral cortex tell us what to see, what to hear, and what to feel. We can screen out unpleasant stimuli to such an extent that they don't reach our conscious awareness.

If we do not have to listen to every loud sound, neither do we have to listen to every rude word. If the sensors of the brain can screen out superfluous material, the intelligence of the brain can screen out unwanted material. We do not need to allow every person who trespasses on our life space to get a hearing from our emotional or rational forces.

The other day as I was driving, I wanted to make a left turn. A woman was in the crosswalk, so I stopped to let her go by. The driver behind me evidently did not see the woman walking in front of me and honked her horn. I glanced in my rearview mirror just in time to see her make an obscene gesture at me. Then she swerved around me to pass and nearly ran over the bewildered pedestrian.

I stewed and fussed about this all afternoon. I told myself not to respond to this rude driver, but I allowed myself to focus too strongly on the event and let it fire up my emergency alarm system.

I'm getting a little better. Instead of reacting like this every week, I now do so only once every two or three months. I am learning that *I decide* who has bugging privileges and who does not. It's a wonderful feeling to learn how to be in charge of my emotions.

You do not have to respond to a rude, aggressive person who cuts in front of you in line. You can say to yourself, "Cool it. Save your emotional energy for someone more worthy."

When loved ones give you a rough time, make allowances. Perhaps they had a bad day at the office or school and are displacing that frustration on you. The more a person loves you, the more verbally careless he or she is apt to be. Refuse to allow yourself to be bugged by every frivolous word. Don't let critical stimuli choose for you; choose your responses.

Listen for the truth

If the devil himself were criticizing you, there probably would be some shred of truth in what he said. So make some attempt to find the truth, the honest thrust behind the angry word. If the criticism is partly justified, then perhaps it can help you. If the criticism is completely unfair, then why bother with something that has no value?

As a music teacher I was once preparing a student for the district music festival. I was telling the girl playing the piano that she needed to put more dynamics and contrast into her playing. Her mother overheard my exhortation and said, "Can't you say anything good to the child? Don't you realize how hard she has practiced? And how brilliant she is for her age? Must you berate her so?"

My feelings were hurt. But later on, I thought the mother had expressed some truth. From then on, when I urged my students to improve, I was careful also to compliment them for the improvements they made.

Do not allow the harsh voice of your critics to scare you away from that portion of truth they have to offer.

Accept yourself—your weaknesses and strengths

One of the best ways to handle unfair criticism or criticism that is only partly true is to jump the gun on your critics and criticize yourself. Chapter 5 was written to help you not criticize yourself as if you were your own enemy, picking on every little thing. But to be realistic, we must be aware of our own failings and accept them. When you quickly and emphatically admit your failings, you take the advantage away from the critic.

Achievement and fulfillment are garnered by those who overcome problems and weaknesses. There is no other way. No one can be the most successful business person, artist, musician, all wrapped up into one. It is rumored that Albert Einstein, even though he conceived the theory of relativity, could not figure his own income tax.

So you have a few weaknesses. Accept them along with your strengths. No matter how you see yourself, God loves you and accepts you, so you can love and accept yourself. The Bible says, "While we were still sinners, Christ died for us" (Romans 5:8). You can say to yourself, "I am not perfect, but I am me." When the critics point out your imperfections, laugh and say, "Yes, I know." Then they may laugh too.

Be grateful for what you have

If you are thankful and grateful for what you have, it is difficult for a critic to take anything away from you. Probably the most important way to keep from being destroyed by critics is to develop a sense of appreciation. Thank God for your gift of life. Be overwhelmed in gratitude for everything you have, and the critic will seem hardly worth the time of day.

Destructive critics are like thieves—they can take away your self-confidence, your achievement, and your personality. One of the ways you can preserve these precious commodities is by strongly tying them to your character with bonds of gratitude. If you are grateful for your achievements, someone who criticizes cannot steal them from you.

We tend to become the object of our attention. If we focus on what the critics say, we tend to become who they say we are. If we focus our attention on the good things we do, the good things tend to grow. One solid way of giving attention to anything is to be thankful for it.

If we give too much attention to a negative event, we make that negative event grow beyond its importance. A pimple can become as significant as a heart transplant if talked about enough. When people say false words about us and we continually rehash what they say, using emotional energy in defensiveness and resistance, we make the negative statements more important than they need to be.

Too much response increases the stimuli. One of the best ways to get a boost from criticism is to refrain from giving criticism a boost. Count your curses, the words of your critics, and you will exacerbate criticism to that place where it will destroy your happiness. Count your blessings. Be grateful, and you will be boosted by your blessings.

Choose when to answer

One day I graciously pointed out to a friend that a price tag was still visible on a new dress she bought. I thought it was better that I called it to her attention than if someone else snickered about it. Fifteen minutes later I was still listening to the explanation as to why the price tag was still on that dress. My pointing out the price tag was an insignificant thing, requiring nothing from her but perhaps, "Thank you," and then we could have gone on to some other business. Some things can be taken care of quietly without much noise.

If the criticism contains some truth, you are not obligated to defend every wrong or purported wrong you ever did.

▧ Summary

Aesop told of an old man and his young son who decided to go to the fair. They took their donkey, their supplies, and the goods they were going to sell at the fair, and off they went.

It was a beautiful day, and they were cheerful until they met a girl who said, "What is a donkey for, but to ride?" So the man put the boy on the donkey's back, along with the boy's knapsack and the goods for the fair.

After a while, they met some men. One of them said, "Now, I call that a sin for the boy to make his poor father walk. Why, I'll bet that boy's too lazy to walk." So the father told the boy to get off the donkey, and he got on.

They had not gone much farther when they met a woman who said, "Shame on that good-for-nothing man to ride while his little boy walks. Has he no pride?" Though the man's feelings were bruised, he lifted the boy and placed him also on the donkey.

Before long they passed a crowd that began to jeer and shout at them. "You must not care what evil you do to load a poor donkey with two such as you."

By the time the man and his son arrived at the fair, they were carrying the donkey upside down with his feet strapped to a pole. Everyone hooted at this spectacle.

On the journey of life, we meet many critics. No matter how pleasant the day, no matter how carefully we have planned our work, someone always has a different idea. If you listen to everything that everyone says, you will end up looking as foolish as Aesop's old man who carried his donkey to the fair.

Instead, evaluate the criticism and learn from it if you can. Then be grateful for what you have, and let your blessings boost you toward your own goals.

9
Dealing with Gossip and Slander

Criticism, with its potential for damage, often disguises itself as gossip. Like a benign tumor that can turn into malignant cancer, gossip slides easily from innocence to guilt. Gossip can be one of the malignant forces that destroys trust and interpersonal relationships. The Bible warns about the danger of idle talk that can lead to gossip, and it frowns on a gossiper who gets joy in life by passing on bad news.

Like criticism, gossip can be extremely harmful, but unlike criticism, which is usually done face to face, gossip is done behind a person's back. Many times, a destructive character assassination comes under the guise of friendly gossip. Sometimes people insidiously hide their malice by joking or pretending to be concerned about a juicy bit of unconfirmed bad news. Gossip can even enter a prayer meeting, when other people's failings are aired and then the gossipers piously declare, "Let us pray for them."

Gossip is the spreading of bad news, true or untrue, about a person with the intent of doing harm or for the perverse pleasure of circulating evil. Some people think that if they tell the truth, it isn't gossip. They ignore the factor of motive. Why are they telling this so-called truth? Will it help anyone? Is it the truth in love? Or is it simply emphasizing the seamy side of life for the purpose of wallowing in muck without receiving blame? Have you ever considered the possibility that enjoying bad news might be as sinful as creating it?

The control of gossip follows the same general principle as criticism: we are to speak the truth in love. When we speak about others, since the other person is not there to defend himself or herself, we must be even more careful to speak the truth. We are to take particular care that the so-called truth we are exchanging with someone else is passed on only for the purpose of helping. The cowardly practice of picking on those not present cannot be excused, even under the banner of prayer.

My first suggestion about gossip is the same as in giving criticism—don't! If you hear some evil news about a person, unless it is confirmed and verified by two or three witnesses, don't believe it. If it is certifiably true, don't pass it on unless you can confidently see that passing on that bad news will help the person you are talking about.

I have an Arabian poem called "Three Gates" that I quote to myself before I speak:

> If you are tempted to reveal
> A tale to you someone has told
> About another, make it pass,
> Before you speak, three gates of gold.

Such narrow gates: First, *"Is it true?"*
Then, *"Is it needful?"* In your mind
Give truthful answer. And the next
Is last and narrowest, *"Is it kind?"*

And if to reach your lips at last
It passes through these gateways three,
Then you may tell the tale, nor fear
What the result of speech may be.

What not to do when you are the object of gossip

Gossip can be a source of pain. If it is a source of pain for you, here are some things to remember.

Don't search for the source of the gossip

First of all, seldom will it be beneficial to hunt down the source of the gossip and correct the bad news. A person who gossips is either ignorant or malicious. If the gossip comes from a person who lies, he or she will also lie about the gossiping. When you approach a person who gossips maliciously, you merely give them something else to gossip about.

Gossip has a way of bouncing around from person to person so that no one really knows who started it. Everyone thinks they heard it from someone else. Also, if you take the trouble to search for the source of the gossip, you make people believe they have actually hit on something important. When you search for the source of gossip, you only stir it up and make it worse.

Don't try to correct it

It is no good to try to collect feathers from a pillow emptied into the wind. Neither will it do any good to try to right all the nasty stories that have been spread to far places by the evil wind of gossip.

Gossip is sin, and like all sin, it has a peculiar trait. The more attention you give to it, the faster it grows. So when you are constantly trying to correct misinformed people, instead of quieting them, you actually accelerate the gossip.

Another disadvantage is that as you try to correct what others might think about you, you will be amazed by the number of people who never heard the story, or if they did hear the story, didn't focus on it enough to remember it. Your attempt to correct their misimpression only reinforces the gossip. When we hear gossip about ourselves, let us not be guilty of being the ones who perpetuate it. Left alone, most gossip dies a natural death. In fact, since gossip is sick, it dies faster than good news.

Don't be defensive

If the bad things that people are saying about you are not true, do not overly defend yourself. Too much defense seems like a sign of guilt. Shakespeare has a line, "The lady doth protest too much, methinks," which suggests she is trying to cover something up.

This truth is illustrated in Guy de Maupassant's story, "A Piece of String." On his way to town on market day a peasant saw a little piece of string lying on the road. Since he was thrifty, he leaned over to pick it up. As he did, he noticed his old enemy, the harness maker, was watching him. The peasant thought to himself, "He will think I am miserly to pick up a little piece of string out of the dirt." He hid the string in his coat and pretended to be looking for something he couldn't find.

Later that day the town crier announced that the purse of a rich man had been lost along the road. A reward was offered for the return of the purse. The harness maker went to the mayor and accused the peasant of having picked up the missing purse and hiding it in his shirt.

When summoned before the mayor, the peasant protested, "Oh, no, it was just a little piece of string." But no one believed him. Even after someone else found the purse, the townspeople still thought the peasant had been involved. This so bothered the peasant that everywhere he went, he loudly defended himself, declaring, "It was just a piece of string." The more he said it, the more the people clacked their tongues and knowingly nudged each other. The truth is that too much defense appears to be a sign of guilt.

Don't retaliate

To gossip back because someone has gossiped about you is not likely to stop the prairie fire. It is likely to burn down some fruitful fields.

You cannot be certain who is actually passing on the stories with malice. Sometimes a well-intentioned person will tell you that John Doe said some malicious thing about you. If you then proceed to bad-mouth John Doe, that "well-intentioned" person is quite likely to tell John Doe what you said. And if John Doe is actually guiltless, you have become the starter of gossip about an innocent person.

The real villain was the reporter. If later on you start to gossip about the "well-intentioned" reporter, he or she will immediately cry out, "I tried to do you good, and you did me harm." You just can't win by gossiping. (That also applies to those who gossip about you; they don't win either.)

Don't become bitter

If we become bitter, resentful, or hateful because of gossip, we harm ourselves. The only thing worse than a person whose character has been assassinated by gossip is a *bitter* person whose character has been assassinated by gossip. Not only that, but when you become bitter, you are actually, on some level, believing the gossip about yourself.

I know a man who was a faithful, honorable Christian, a deacon in the church. Some malicious people started a gossip campaign, claiming the deacon had a police record and was guilty of sexual misconduct. The gossips did not ask the deacon whether he had a police record. They just assumed that another person with the same name was he. The deacon left the church, and before long, he also lost his faith in God.

A favorite weapon of the devil to get people to leave the church consists of getting good Christian people to pass on harmful gossip. It's even worse when the person who is the object of gossip reacts in a bitter way and uses the sin of gossip as an excuse for rejecting God.

Don't punish yourself

Do not engage in self-punishment by allowing your self-esteem to be damaged by gossip. What people say about you should not be allowed to determine how you feel about yourself. You are God's child, a member of God's family. If you have done something wrong, you will need to seek forgiveness and restitution. To slip under the rug, and let yourself be stepped on by every dirty foot, will not stop the gossips. It will only make them believe that what they have said about you is true. So do not allow other people's habit of gossip to determine your attitude about yourself.

In Nathaniel Hawthorne's *The Scarlet Letter,* a beautiful young woman who was accused of adultery maintained her dignity and honor. Even after being forced to wear a scarlet "A" and receive the scorn and taunts of the village hypocrites, she held her head high, maintained her self-esteem, and protected the identity of her lover, the minister. He, however, who never admitted his guilt, became his own self-critic, lost his self-esteem, and destroyed his effectiveness.

One sin does not justify another. If you have sinned and others gossip about you, do not exacerbate the situation by losing your self-esteem.

What does one do in the face of gossip?

Now that we have explored what not to do when you hear gossip, here are some helpful suggestions about how to handle it.

Change your behavior or accept the gossip

First, ask yourself whether the stories being told about you are true. If so, then change your conduct. If you do not want to change your conduct, accept the news that is being circulated about you without complaint.

Government, societies, and individual people have different concepts of right and wrong. Even in religion, a serious sin in one denomination can be acceptable conduct in another. If you are doing what is unacceptable to a group of people with whom you associate, and they gossip about you, what can you expect? If you are doing something wrong and don't want to change, then be prepared to accept the consequences, one of which is gossip.

The advice is simple: change your unacceptable ways or accept with good grace the natural consequences of people differing with you.

Speak well of yourself

Don't be your own purveyor of bad news. If people are saying bad things about you, don't add to it by saying bad things about yourself. You have enough enemies. The Bible tells us to love our enemies, but it certainly doesn't tell us to *join* them.

Some people never have a good word to say about themselves and then wonder why no one else does either. Do not create your own bad reputation by your own mouth. Speak well of yourself, and other people will too.

Strengthen yourself

When you hear malicious gossip about yourself, become alert, rally your friends, and strengthen your position. An enemy is after you—maybe even the evil one himself. When the accuser is hot on your trail, you need all the strength you can get to ward off his attack on your character.

A woman called me one day and severely criticized me. At first I was deeply hurt and accepted her accusations with feelings of inferiority and guilt. I dropped into a self-pitying depression. Then the still, small voice that God often sends as a protective force to his children came to me and whispered in my ear, "Use this critical gossip to strengthen yourself. Become a better man."

Now, when I hear a word of gossip or a critical report about me, I try to think of it as a message from God telling me it is time to become a little stronger. One of the secrets of greatness is not the elimination of errors but making oneself stronger than the errors.

Use the gossip to motivate yourself

I am amazed at the glory, the majesty, the beauty, and the magnificence of the words of David in the Psalms. Nowhere in all the literature of the world can such inspirational, poetic language be found. Most of it grew out of David's errors, stupidities, and sins. When the people began to gossip about his flagrant disregard for the life of one of his loyal soldiers and his dishonorable relations with that soldier's wife, David made no excuses. Instead, he wrote psalms that became part of the Word of God. Let us decide that our sins, our stupidities, our errors, our little failings will not determine our mental attitude, our self-esteem, or our drive for achievement.

For ten years I worked as a psychologist in a California prison, where many men had lost the vision of life. They had indeed done bad things—they had terrible reputations; they were distrusted, abandoned, rejected, and gossiped about. But the real problem was that they believed in their bad nature. No matter how much good they had accomplished, the good was nullified by what other people thought. I tried to persuade those men to believe in good, and in God, and to allow the good to motivate them to run the race of life successfully.

The best way to meet criticism is to consider it a prod that can motivate you. When you hear an infuriating word of gossip about yourself, don't let it tear you down. Start immediately to build yourself up. Let bad news give you a good-news boost.

Emphasize good news

With your imagination, with your prayers, with your verbalizations, with your visualizations, and with the energy of your emotions, accept the following truth: God hates bad news, and he asks us to completely reject the evil one whose power comes from bad news. God loves good news, and he invites us to follow him and build his kingdom by spreading the good news of the gospel.

How do we condition our minds to spread good news? First of all, we react with great enthusiasm to all good things. Secondly, we do not react with emotional strength to negative things.

When someone gossips, pay little attention to it. Don't give it strength by responding with emotional shock, exclamatory words, heavy-handed action, or anxiety and worry. Save your thoughts, emotions, and actions for the wonderful, beautiful, glorious things of God. Concentrate on good news and let it motivate you.

Pray for those who gossip about you

Jesus said, "Love your enemies and pray for those who persecute you, that you may be sons of your Father in heaven" (Matthew 5:44-45). When people gossip about us and say harmful things to put us down, our usual reaction is to get angry, to defend ourselves, and to strike back. It seems almost natural to fight back, but it doesn't work. The harder we fight, the worse it gets. Jesus said, "Bless those who curse you" (Luke 6:28). This means, speak well of those people who say bad things about you. Good news spreads even more than bad news. If you speak well of your critics, they may hear about it—and stop the gossip.

When someone is your enemy, pray for, bless, and do good to him or her, and before long, that enemy will have become your friend. And if the person does not become your friend, who in this world can possibly respect the person who is saying evil about someone who speaks only good in return? And when one hears ill-natured gossip about a third person, one can always respond: "What a pity you are at odds with her! She always speaks so well of you." Use good news to overpower bad news.

■ Summary

Gossip can be one of the worst things ever to happen to a

person, or it can be one of the best things. When we stumble over a rock, sometimes we awaken the life force, alert the mind power, and motivate the soul energy to watch where we are going and turn stumbling blocks into stepping stones.

We can make gossip a stepping stone by ignoring it as much as possible. We can forgive the gossiper and avoid revenge or bitterness. We can build ourselves up, motivate ourselves, emphasize good news, and pray for the gossipers.

Afterword

Words can be used to destroy people. But words are also the chief means of molding our character. Evil words, however, cannot build good character. Criticism is like the vacuum cleaner which sucks up dirt from the rug of life. Criticism looks at what is wrong, and then with bitterness and sarcasm, calls it to the other person's attention.

Instead of leveling an attack at another person, you can choose to be an encourager. You can choose to be an affirmer. And when correction is necessary, you can criticize without arousing resentment. What a wonderful world this would be if we all worked on alternatives to giving criticism and developed strategies to survive it!

Someone once said, "What we weave in this world we shall wear in heaven." How becoming the garments of affirmation and encouragement will be on us!

Quality Ministry Resources for Caring Congregations

 Other Care Classic® Books

The Promise of Hope:
Coping When Life Caves In
by William Kinnaird

A personal witness of faith and courage. Bill Kinnaird brings a message of hope to those who struggle and suffer. Amid the turmoil of daily life, he offers a place filled with reason, purpose, and the reassurance that God is always there.

Joy Comes with the Morning:
The Positive Power of Christian
Encouragement *by William Kinnaird*

A wealth of personal insights and timeless ideas for Christian caregiving. Whether for daily meditations or study by a group, this book makes real God's love for and through God's people.

Bill Kinnaird's experiences, combined with what he has learned from the Bible and great teachers such as C. S. Lewis and Paul Tournier, speak to the heart of every reader.

Two Ministry Systems from Stephen Ministries®

1. The Stephen Series®

A complete system for training and organizing laypersons for one-to-one caring ministry in their congregations and communities

Congregations from over 75 Christian denominations in the United States and 17 foreign countries are using the Stephen Series to care for hurting people and people in crisis. Since 1975 Stephen Ministries has been committed to maintaining and delivering a quality lay caring ministry system. The Stephen Series IS distinctively Christian caring.

To learn more about the Stephen Series you might want to order one of the following information videos.

THE HEART OF STEPHEN MINISTRY

The heart of Stephen Ministry is "Christ caring for people through people." The stories in this extraordinary ten-minute video show the healing, joy, and renewed lives that God brings through Stephen Ministry—not only for those who receive care but also for those who serve as Stephen Ministers and Stephen Leaders. *The Heart of Stephen Ministry* helps people catch the vision for life-changing lay caring ministry—not only with their eyes, but also with their hearts.

THE GIFT OF STEPHEN MINISTRY

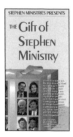

This 20-minute video explains how any congregation can benefit from the many gifts the Stephen Series offers through lay caring ministry. People who have known the gifts of the Stephen Series—pastors, lay leaders, Stephen Ministers, care receivers—share their stories, telling how God has blessed them, changing their lives and giving them hope, and how other congregations can share in those blessings.

2. The ChristCare® Series

A comprehensive system for leading and organizing lay small group ministry that enables congregations to care for the spiritual growth and needs of their members

This complete ministry system offers congregations the opportunity to build Christian community through small groups by helping members care for one another, engage in Biblical Equipping, join together in prayer and worship, and extend themselves outward to help others through missional activity. Carefully researched and extensively tested, the ChristCare Series offers a detailed, well-integrated system for developing and delivering a small group ministry that works.

To learn more about the ChristCare Series you might want to order the following information video.

THE CHRISTCARE SERIES AT WORK
This 20-minute video describes ChristCare Group Ministry through the words of those who know it best—the pastors and other leaders who are directing this system of small group ministry in their congregations. This presentation helps pastoral groups—boards, committees, even the congregation as a whole—understand the ChristCare Series, why this system of small group ministry works, and how this system can further spiritual growth and community within individual congregations.

Courses from Stephen Ministries

CARING EVANGELISM: HOW TO LIVE AND SHARE CHRIST'S LOVE

A 16-hour course that equips Christians to be caring evangelists in their daily lives

This is evangelism training for people who never thought they could be evangelists. Course materials include the *Leader's Guide, Participant Manual*, and *Administrative Handbook*. Participants read the book *Me, an Evangelist? Every Christian's Guide to Caring Evangelism.* Developed over a period of five years, the course equips God's people to fulfill the Great Commission.

CARING FOR INACTIVE MEMBERS: HOW TO MAKE GOD'S HOUSE A HOME

Designed for use by church staff, lay leaders, and members

This course on church inactivity provides a comprehensive congregational approach to inactive member ministry. Ten to 14 hours of course work address the issues of preventing inactivity, caring for inactive members, and welcoming inactive members back to God's house. Participants learn a caring approach to an often sensitive situation. Course includes the *Leader's Guide, Participant Manual*, and text, *Reopening the Back Door: Answers to Questions about Ministering to Inactive Members.*

ANTAGONISTS IN THE CHURCH

A course on how to identify and deal with destructive conflict

This practical course helps participants identify and deal with church members who attack leaders and destroy ministry. The book *Antagonists in the Church* and the companion *Study Guide* teach participants how to recognize, prevent, confront, and halt antagonists in the church.

CHRISTIAN CAREGIVING—
A WAY OF LIFE

**The definitive approach to
distinctively Christian care**

Based on the *Christian Caregiving—a Way of Life* book and the accompanying *Christian Caregiving—a Way of Life Leader's Guide*, this 20-hour course answers many questions about putting faith into action. Participants learn how to use Christian resources, such as prayer and the Bible, in their everyday caring and relating. Distinctively Christian caring really can be a way of life!

DISCOVERING GOD'S VISION FOR YOUR LIFE: YOU AND YOUR SPIRITUAL GIFTS

An 8-hour course designed to help members discover their gifts and mobilize them for ministry

This complete set of resources, including a *Leader's Guide* and *Participant Manual*, helps congregation members understand their own spiritual gifts for ministry, gives them a solid foundation in the theology of Christian ministry and discipleship, and motivates them to use their spiritual gifts in service to others. Additional resources help congregation members prepare for the course and put the findings to practical use in ministry afterward.

For more information about these and other ministry resources, contact:

Stephen Ministries
2045 Innerbelt Business Center Drive
St. Louis, MO 63114-5765
Phone: 314/428-2600   Fax: 314/428-7888